Re-Architecting Thought Process & Sexual Behavior

Re-Architecting Thought Process & Sexual Behavior

Editor

Gyanesh G. Sharma

SCHOOL OF LIFE MANAGEMENT

Transforming life through self-refinement

Published by
School of Life Management
E-143, Lajpat Nagar, Sahibabad,
Distt. Ghaziabad, UP – 201005, India
www.schooloflifemanagement.org

Co-Published by
COPAL Publishing Group
E-143, Lajpat Nagar, Sahibabad,
Distt. Ghaziabad, UP – 201005, India
www.copalpublishing.com

First Published 2016
© School of Life Management and COPAL Publishing, 2016

ISBN: 978-93-83419-32-6 (hard back)
ISBN: 978-93-83419-33-3 (e-book)

Typeset by Bhumi Graphics, New Delhi
Printed and bound by Bhavish Graphics, Chennai

Preface

"In day-to-day battle of conflicting thoughts and life's challenges, inspirational books act as weapons."

What separates us from other species is the presence of 'Thought' and 'Compassion' in every human being. Unfortunately, with growing materialism and living standards, human thought is losing its direction and emotions are drying from core of the heart. Man is trying to achieve satisfaction through technological innovations and prosperity but dearth of quality thinking and empathy is causing health problems, mental stress, dissatisfaction, conflict, and social problems as compared to past times.

On deeper analysis, what I concluded is the erosion of human sentiments and mismanagement of thought process behind all such agonies. Obscenity and pornography is further extension to wrong choices of modern civilization. Porn at home and work place poses devastating effects on human character, the building block of a descent society.

Advancement in IT sector has brought world closer but lack of regulation on explicit materials on Internet is leading to uncontrolled growth of pornography. Like child playing with a loaded gun, pornography is affecting sexual behaviour of youngsters arousing sexual urge pre-maturely. Upsurge of pornography is not only objectifying women's image but idealizing acts of aggression, hostility, furtive and unnatural sex.

This book gives precise information about risks associated with pornography and advocates for providing sex education to aware adolescents on sexual issues. Sex education is considered as globally accepted solution to guide teens as they undergo change in sex organs, feelings towards opposite sex and prepare for sex life. However, ignorance of parents and educational institutions as well as social and religious believes has blocked the scope of providing sex education in many countries.

Education is incomplete without incorporating values. Spiritual science is precious gift of ancient Rishis and it has immense power to transform and encourage its true follower. The reader of this book will get acquainted with life management skills supported by scientific and practical methods. Developing strong will power, maintaining good relationship and sound health are few traits of spirituality that reforms character, the foundation of sexual life.

I hope this book will prove helpful in developing cardinal virtues of faith and confidence for noble art of living.

Gyanesh G. Sharma

Dr. Pranav Pandya MD (Medicine)
Chancellor Dev Sanskriti Vishwavidyalaya
Head All World Gayatri Pariwar
Director Brahmavarchas Research Institute
Editor Akhand Jyoti (Monthly Magazine in 8 Languages)

DEV SANSKRITI
VISHWAVIDYALAYA

27th August 2015

Foreword

I am pleased to note that Shri Gyanesh G. Sharma and Shri Sumit Aggarwal have written this book titled 'Re-Architecting Thought Process & Sexual Behavior', focused on various extremely relevant topics of the present times like sex education, dangers of pornography and life management as a tool for self transformation. The society is struggling with the ill effects of pornography, and under such circumstances different techniques of life management based on ancient spiritual wisdom are the only recourse. I am sure that this book will serve as a useful guide in this regard.

I convey my heartiest best wishes to the authors for this noble endeavor of serving the humanity.

(Dr. Pranav Pandya)

Gayatrikunj - Shantikunj, Haridwar - 249411 (Uttarakhand)
Phone: +91-1334-260602, 260309, 260723, 261367 • Fax: +91-1334-260866
Email: shantikunj@awgp.org • Website: www.dsvv.ac.in | www.awgp.org

Acknowledgement

Thanks to my respected spiritual master Pandit Sriram Sharma Acharya, who inspired and enabled me to research on such an important issue posing threat to ethical standards of today's youth.

I submit my heartiest gratitude to members of All World Gayatri Pariwar, who are always with me to guide and support selfless work for humanity irrespective of caste, religion and nationality.

I revere the patronage and moral support extended by my parents whose passionate encouragement made it possible to complete this book.

I extend my thanks to my wife Pragya for her co-operation and support in completing this project.

I am thankful to Lalit Rawat, Graphic Designer, for his sincere help in creating this book.

I humbly extend my thanks to readers of this book for dedicating precious time in acknowledging social issues and importance of moral values.

Though I have tried my best to provide sources of information from books, websites and research publications but if any reference is missed unintentionally, I acknowledge the same.

Gyanesh G. Sharma

Dedicated to...

Every individual engaged in selfless service to mankind making
Mother Earth a peaceful and safe place for human existence.

Contributors

A research scholar and activist, **Seema Sharma** is working for rights of women and children and provides training on development of effective life management skills. Her objective is to empower every individual with righteous thought to enable him face diverse challenges in life. Seema considers that self-refinement is the basis of global peace and harmony. She provides motivational training to teachers, students and parents in various topics of self-development.

Seema uses scientific theories to validate significance of ancient spiritual theories and its positive effects on human mind and behaviour. Seema's altruistic endeavors and scientific approach to spiritual awakening is source of inspiration for today's young generation because modernisation and values, together can make nation respectful and strong.

An entrepreneur and motivator, **Sumit Aggarwal** is a committed social reformer with aim of transforming moribund human institutions into healthy, happy and progressive society based on moral convictions.

Sumit is an active member of All World Gayatri Pariwar and involved in resolving problems of illiteracy, drug addiction and obscenity in the society. He encourages young people to invest their time and talent in self-refinement and altruism to enlighten their intellect.

Sumit believes that root cause of growing stress and mental agony in youth is failure to realise true significance of spiritual science in our daily life. Today, man is focusing on progress of mind and body but has discarded the soul. Now, it is high time to inculcate collective aspiration to achieve idealistic excellence, peace and prosperity.

Contents

Part III : The Unique Art of Life Management

Media Reports on Pornography Risks and Sex Education

'Parents should not shy away from discussing sex with children'

Porn Ban No Deterrent, Say Psychiatrists

Namita.Devidayal@timesgroup.com

In a world which is spinning faster than you can say pop up, adolescents are particularly fraught. Whether or not the government ban on pornography websites is justified, parents continue to be concerned about the easy access to inappropriate material on the digital devices that are attached to most children like additional body parts.

Recently, a 13 year old at a prestigious international school caught his teacher's attention because of his unnaturally frequent trips to the toilet. She finally followed him and caught the young boy and a friend riveted to an adult website on his smart phone. The school has since come up with a strict policy on students and their cyber devices. But parents and school authorities are aware that the issue is far more pervasive, and often beyond their control.

Counsellors, especially those who work with adolescents, suggest watching porn is a part of normal adolescent curiosity and a ban is likely to increase interest rather than act as a deterrent. Rather, they advise parents to be less squeamish with their children when discussing sexuality.

If a child is reprimanded for watching porn, he or she is likely to equate sex with sin and shame, which can lead to sexual disorders later.

"I am not that alarmed that kids are watching porn," says psychiatrist Pervin Dadachanji. "But I am alarmed at what is available today. There is violence, there is exploitation, there may be things like a man having sex with a virgin, showing her crying."

"Parents could explain to their children that the porn industry is like WWE (World Wrestling Entertainment), that it is all stunts and rigged, it is not real," adds Dadachanji.

She says children should be advised to differentiate between what they are watching and the real act of making love.

HOW TO KEEP TABS

Cyber-security consultant Tapan Mehta advises parents on how to monitor the parallel digital world that their children inhabit

> Become tech-savvy and at least know the basics of the internet, such as how to block sites or pop-ups through the browser

> Be aware of online social networking websites where the most bullying takes place. You can see your kids' friends in the building and school, but online you have no idea who they are. People commonly fake profiles, pretending to be a young person

> Ensure that any online game is age-appropriate. For example, 'clash of clans' is a perfectly decent game, but there are people chatting live and they could be using inappropriate sexual language

> If you receive adult pictures or videos on your phone, make sure they are not saved in your library, because a child may casually access your phone while it is charging or lying around

> Talk openly to a child on how certain online sites can affect their off-line lives

Periodically check browsing history, both on the child's phone and computer

This is an industry. It's not even about sex or feelings. In some cases, women are exploited in the videos. Children can identify with exploitation, so if you explain that to them, they will understand," she adds.

The ubiquitous access through phones, computers and other digital devices is the biggest cause for concern, say counsellors. Applications like 'WhatsApp' enable images and videos to be passed around far more gratuitously than, say, sharing a Playboy magazine, or getting together to watch a nudie vid or once in a while, which happened in "the good old days".

Today, with the internet as the primary source for virtually everything, adult material often pops up randomly, even if a child isn't looking for it.

As consultant psychiatrist Kersi Chavda says, "I've had kids who said they were doing research on snakes on the net, and when they typed in 'black snake', they were confronted with a pop-up which led them to an African American pornography site. When a child is not even looking and gets thrust in his face, that is certainly something that should be avoided."

However, Chavda is very clear that indulging in pornography once in a while is not seen to cause problems. "If a child is brought up on a natural diet of sexuality, then the chances of his becoming sensible towards sexuality are far more. Even if he occasionally indulges in porn, it is unlikely it will become the focus of his life.

"On the other hand, a person who is very restricted, who has very little access, if suddenly flooded with an onslaught of sexual images, will probably end up thinking that that is normal. Fantasy will take over reality. It will lead to abnormal sexual behaviour." Asked about the age he considers it 'normal' for a child to explore porn, he says that 14 to 16 years should not raise eyebrows.

Cyber security expert Tapan Mehta says that adults have no choice but to become tech-savvy if they are giving their children access to computers and smartphones.

"All parents should understand the basics of the internet and be able to periodically check the child's browsing history. There is a simple way of going on to the internet browser settings and blocking all pop-ups," says Mehta, who routinely speaks at schools, alerting both children and parents on the need to be vigilant.

"The bigger problem is the phone. While you can control computers, and keep them in a public place in the home, it is very difficult to control phones," he says. "The pop-ups are usually blocked by the service provider, but they do show up. Much better to talk to the child openly about all these things. Sex education is a must."

Abortions by U-15 Mum girls up 67%

'Rise Indicates Need To Talk About Teen Sex'

Sumitra.DebRoy@timesgroup.com

Mumbai: Abortions among teenage girls below the age of 15 in Mumbai have recorded an alarming 67% spike in 2014-15. Civic data accessed through an RTI further shows that out of nearly 31,000 women who opted for medical termination of pregnancy, 1,600 were below the age of 19.

Health experts have called the trend of unwanted pregnancies alarming, while harping on the need for better sex education in schools and junior colleges. The BMC data, collated from all licenced Medical Termination of Pregnancy (MTP) centres in the city, shows that in 2013-14 around 111 girls below the age of 15 had undergone an abortion. The number has risen to 185 in 2014-15. Even for the age-bracket of 15-19, there has been a 47% jump when compared with the previous year.

Interestingly, Andheri east and west emerged as the abortion centres, reporting nearly 6,000 cases. Civic officials have attributed the increase to better and more accurate reporting.

Social and health pundits, however, also hinted at the possibility of young girls being exploited as well as the prevalence of under-age marriages in Indian society. A senior doctor from a civic hospital said, "Teenage pregnancies are becoming common, though most prefer to get it done in private set-ups for privacy issues."

"The numbers are shocking," said gynaecologist and former president of Federation of Obstetric and Gynaecological Societies of India Dr Suchitra Pandit. "What is worrisome is these girls are just out of school. On one hand, we have more and more young girls walking up to doctors and asking for contraceptives, and on the other we have these statistics," she added. Pandit believes the reasons vary from curiosity to exploitation to plain ignorance about safe sex. An analysis of reasons why women needed MTPs (carried out in 2013-14) showed that failure of contraceptives topped the chart, with nearly 23,000 out of 30,000 stating it. The other reasons shown were danger to mother's life or that the child may suffer from abnormalities. In only 10 cases, rape was shown as the reason for pregnancy.

However, others feel it is time for planners to device smarter ways to reach out to the young rather than brushing the issue under the carpet. "There is increased sexual activity among teenagers. Sex is happening everywhere but nobody wants to talk about it," said Nayreen Daruwalla, who heads the NGO SNEHA's centre for vulnerable women and children.

MEDICAL TERMINATION OF PREGNANCY

Abortions in City Over The Years

Year	Cases	Deaths
2014-15	30,742	0
2013-14	30,117	3
2012-13	27,256	8
2011-12	17,309	23

What The Law Says

> Abortions can only be performed in a public hospital or a place approved for the purpose by the authorities

> Termination of pregnancy by an unregistered medical practitioner is an offence punishable with rigorous imprisonment of two to seven years

> MTP is legally allowed only till the 20th week of pregnancy in India

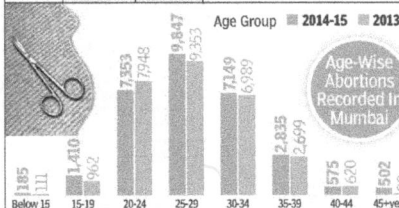

Age Group ■ 2014-15 ■ 2013-14

Age Group	2014-15	2013-14
Below 15	185	111
15-19	1,410	962
20-24	7,353	7,948
25-29	9,847	9,353
30-34	7,149	6,989
35-39	2,835	2,699
40-44	575	620
45+years	502	90

Age-Wise Abortions Recorded In Mumbai

'Experiments with sex on the rise'

▶Continued from P1

Among those surveyed, over 6.5% boys and over 1.3% girls reported to have had intercourse at least once. The average age at first intercourse in those who had it was 15.25 years for boys and 16.66 years for girls," it added. The National Family Health Survey 3, which car... 2006, said that youn... aged between 16 an... monly engage in pr... sex, more men (15-22... women (1.6%).

Well-known sexolo... M Watsa said the survey... ings corroborate what... studies have sh... shown. "The SE... STD-affected numbers seem huge. Given dia's population, even 4% huge number," he said.

Amita Dhanu of the Fam... Planning Association of In... (FPA) said sexual experimen... tation is on the rise among In... dia's youth. "Younger boys ex... periment with sex and younger girls want to experiment with premarital sex. Although there are instances of date rapes and molestation, there is also a new trend of girls willing to experiment," she said, add... ing that the number of girls coming with complaints that their boyfriends coerced them into having sex has fallen.

The area of concern here is the inadequate awareness of STDs and prevention. "Use of contraceptives is almost nil in this age group," said Dhanu.

Dr Rajan Bhonsale, head of the sexual medicine depart- ment of BMC-run KEM Hospi- tal, Parel, said today's lifestyle

encourages reckless acts. "There is a growing incidence of HIV among affluent teenag- ers because they have multi- ple partners," said Bhonsale.

The latest survey provides a reason for the increase in STDs among teenagers: No proper communication chan... nels to gain e...

PRICE ₹5.00 OR ₹9.50 WITH SUNDAY NAVBHARAT TIMES

City kids now have their 1st brush with sex at 14, says study

9% Contract STDs, Up From 4% in 2011

Malathy.Iyer@timesgroup.com

Mumbai: Here is one more reason why the government should offer sex education: Indian teens are not only sexually active at a younger age than before, more are contracting sexually trans- mitted infections as well.

A survey, based on inter- views of 15,000-odd teens be- tween 13 and 19 years from eight metros and 12 cities, re- vealed that the average age at first sexual contact for boys was 13.72 years and 14.1 for girls. Around 8.9% said they had contracted a sexually transmitted infec- tion at least once. The figure was just 4% in 2011-12.

'MANY PARTNERS'

➤ 30.08% boys and 17.18% girls have sexual contact before 20

➤ Avg age of 1st intercourse: 15.25 for boys and 16.66 for girls

➤ 6.31% boys and 1.31% girls have premarital sex before 20

> There is a growing incidence of HIV among affluent teenagers because they have multiple partners—**DR RAJAN BHONSALE**
> KEM HOSPITAL, MUMBAI

"This is alarming consid- ering that it's more than dou- ble the STD/HIV incidence reported for this age group in the National AIDS Control Organization annual report of 2011-12," said Dr Debraj Shome of MediAngels.com, an e-healthcare company funded by the department of science and technology, which conducted the survey.

▶'More experiments', P 12

TIMES

Sexting now the norm for teens

Most Say Activity Similar To Taking Selfies, Warns UK Crime Agency

Paul Gallagher

Sexting between teenagers has become the norm, and the Na- tional Crime Agency as it launched a campaign on Monday to deal with a surge in cases of children sharing sexually explicit images and video.

The Agency's Child Exploitation and Online Protection Centre (CE- OP) said it receives reports of young people sending self-generated nude or nearly nude visuals on a daily ba- sis. Typical cases include someone receiving an explicit private mess- age before forwarding it on to others — a revealing image being posted on a website or social media with low pri- vacy settings, or a young person be- ing blackmailed by a stranger over revealing images they have been tricked into taking.

In-depth interviews were carried out with 11 young people in the UK and Sweden to discover not only why they send explicit content, but what it means to them, the impact of engag- ing in this behaviour and the advice to others. Many of those interviewed could...

DANGEROUS TREND

one they were in a relationship with into sending explicit images.

Ethel Quayle, project leader and senior lecturer in clinical psycho- gy at the University of Edinburgh, said the group's findings have been turned into practical advice. "It is not about condoning the activity, rather it is about providing more practical advice about being able to talk about this and manage issues when they come about," she said. "It is interest- ing that the majority of young people we interviewed didn't refer once to 'sexting'. Instead they saw this as 'in- gry selfies or nude selfies.'

Zoe Hilton, head of safeguarding at the NCA's CEOP Command, said: "Children and young people don't nec- essarily know that sexting is danger- ous. It can start off on a bit of fun but the issue can start when that image gets into the wrong hands." THE INDEPENDENT

THE INDEPENDENT Friday 10 AUGUST 2015

NEWS   VIDEO   PEOPLE   VOICES   SPORT   TECH   LIFE   PROPERTY   ARTS + ENTS   TRAVEL

'How to rape a woman': People searching for rape porn end up on sexual abuse investigation website

ADAM WITHNALL   Thursday 09 January 2014

f SHARE   TWEET   G+ SHARE   REDDIT   in SHARE

An organisation which investigates sexual abuse of women has discovered that a large number of the visitors to its website appear to be arriving looking for porn or advice on 'how to rape women'.

The director of Women Under Siege was able to look at the search terms used by people coming to the site, and has revealed for the first time the shocking list of Google searches through which rapists and rape fantasists end up finding their articles.

Lauren Wolfe, the journalist who runs Women Under Siege, said she was investigating how people came to read a recent piece entitled "Women in South Africa are living in a war zone".

The Washington Post

Opinions

Child pornography: Who should pay?

A   🖶   💬 52

By Arjun Sethi

Arjun Sethi is a lawyer in Washington. He is on Twitter @arjunsethi83

At the ages of 8 and 9, a woman described in court documents as Amy Unknown was raped by her uncle and forever turned into a pornographic image. Now, more than 15 years later, her pictures are among the most widely disseminated child pornography in the world. There is a global market for her images, and they have been implicated in thousands of cases worldwide.

Amy experiences re-victimization because her abuse is perpetual. Many of her images will never be recovered, and closure seems unlikely, if not impossible. In her own words: "Every day of my life I live in constant fear that someone will see my pictures and recognize me and that I will be humiliated all over again."

5 The Washington Post

PART I
SEX EDUCATION: GUIDANCE FOR ADOLESCENTS, TEACHERS AND PARENTS

Why You Need Sex Education

Sex education refers to instruction on a wide range of issues relating to human sexuality such as sexual anatomy, reproduction, sexual intercourse, reproductive health, safe sex practices, reproductive rights and responsibilities, abstinence, contraception, and other aspects of human sexual behavior. Traditionally, adolescents in many cultures were not given any information on sexual matters, with the discussion of these issues being considered taboo. Lack of healthy discussion on sexuality at homes and schools lead teenagers

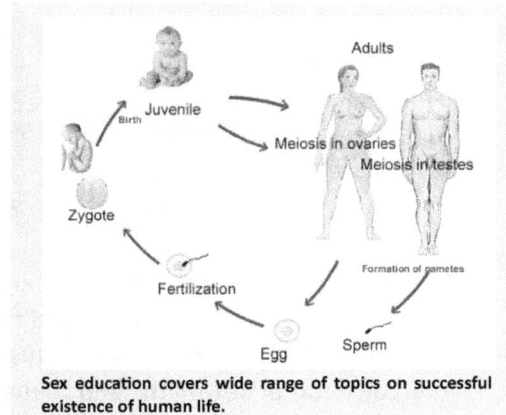

Sex education covers wide range of topics on successful existence of human life.

to get information from friends and media, and much of this information was deficient or dubious value, especially during the period following puberty when curiosity about sexual matters was the most acute. Increasing incidence of teenage pregnancies and outbreak of AIDS has given a new sense of urgency to sex education.

Currently, few young people are receiving proper sex education which leaves them vulnerable to coercion, abuse, exploitation, unintended pregnancy and sexually transmitted infections, including HIV. The UNAIDS 2008 Global Report on the AIDS Epidemic reported that only 40% of young people aged 15–24 had accurate knowledge about HIV and transmission. This knowledge is all the more urgent as young people aged 15-24 account for 45% of all new HIV infections. School settings provide an important opportunity to reach large numbers of young people with sex education before they become sexually active, as well as offering an appropriate structure within which to do so.

Sex education provides guidance to teenagers to develop skills for building strong and healthy relationships, dealing with sexual problems, and maintaining good physical and mental health. As teens undergo period of puberty, hormones bring changes as body prepares for sexual reproduction. Sex education helps teens to understand need of delaying sex, avoiding unwanted pregnancy, protection from sexually transmitted diseases, body image, safe sex practices and dealing with sexual abuse.

Benefits of Sex Education to Teenagers

○ **Protect from health risks:** Children are unaware about consequences of unsafe sex causing teenage pregnancy, sexually transmitted infections (STIs) affecting overall health. It is estimated that 34 percent of HIV infected persons are teenagers. Not all STIs show early signs and symptoms and easily curable. Some may pose threat to life others are curable by antibiotics.

Schools may provide environment in which teens can discuss sexual issues.

○ **Creates responsible behaviour:** Sex education can help children impact of sex in their lives. Teens can learn sex ethics and adopt responsible behaviour towards friends with opposite sex. Teachers and parents can discuss need for abstinence until marriage. It also helps in eradication of sex myths and teens can be saved from getting inaccurate information regarding sex. It also provides opportunity to understand people with different sexual orientation.

○ **Help prevent teenage pregnancy:** Lack of sex education due to religious or cultural ideologies resulting in rise in teenage pregnancy. According to WHO, children above twelve years of age should be provided sex education. Sex education is best way to guide students about hormonal changes in body and how to tackle sexual excitation in different situations.

○ **Aware youth for safe sex practices:** Sex education at early stage aware teenagers how to deal with changes in sexual behaviour during puberty. Even if teenagers indulge in sex, they could protect themselves from pregnancy or STIs by using condoms or use other safety techniques. In this way, a person can learn science of safe sex before marriage or indulging into sexual intercourse.

○ **Provides frankness in talks on sexual issues:** In today's society, kids are often exposed to explicit materials from Internet or friend circle and if they fail to receive sex education right from the beginning, they could gather this information from other sources. Therefore, it is important for parents to guide them through this. Talking about sex increases confidence in teens and they feel more frank with their elders. Thus early sex education help create strong value system before they have sexual experience.

Know Your Sexual Orientation

A person's sexual orientation, like their blood type, exists whether or not that person knows what to label it. Sexual orientation provides sexual identity of a person based on sexual attraction and related behaviour towards opposite or same sex or gender. These attractions are generally subsumed under heterosexuality, homosexuality, bisexuality and asexuality. Experts believe that combination of genetic, hormonal, prenatal and environmental factors are responsible for change in sexual orientation. For most individuals, a label such as straight, gay, lesbian, bisexual, pansexual, queer, or asexual identifies that person's sexual orientation identity.

Homosexuality: Homosexuality is sexual attraction or related behaviour towards person of same sex or gender. The most common terms for homosexual people are lesbian for females and gay for males. Many gay and lesbian people are in committed same-sex relationships. There has been a global movement towards recognition and legal rights for homosexual people, including the rights to marriage and civil unions, adoption and parenting, employment, military service, equal access to health care etc.

Heterosexuality: Heterosexuality is sexual attraction or related behaviour towards person of opposite sex or gender. Heterosexuality is observed not only in humans but all animals including mammals. Heterosexuality is responsible for sexual reproduction by sexual intercourse between male and female giving rise to birth of offspring.

Bisexuality: Bisexuality is sexual attraction or romantic relationship with people of both sexes, i.e., male and female. Many bisexuals keep their sexual orientation secret, so bisexuals as a group are uncommon in society.

Transgender: Transgender or transsexual people are born with typical male or female anatomies but they feel they were born in the wrong gender. For example, a person who is transgender may have a typical female body but feel like a male and opt to undergo sex reassignment surgeries to become male.

LGBT: LGBT is an initialism which stands for Lesbian, Gay, Bisexual and Transgender. LGBT is intended to emphasize a diversity of sexuality and gender identity-based cultures across the world. LGBT may face challenges in free interactions within a community if your religious and/ or ethnic community tends to view LGBT people and same-sex relationships negatively. To live an authentic life freely and joyfully is an ongoing journey for everyone, regardless of sexual orientation.

Queer: Queer is an umbrella term for sexual and gender minorities that are not heterosexual. Many LGBT people disapprove of using queer because they consider it offensive.

Sexuality is about much more than just sex. It includes:

- ○ Your body, including your sexual and reproductive anatomy and body image — how you feel about your body.

- ○ Your biological sex — male, female, or intersex

- ○ Your gender — being a girl, boy, woman, man, or transgender

- ○ Your gender identity — feelings about and how you express your gender

Sex education empowers you to take right decision on sex, health and relationship.

- ○ Your sexual orientation — who you're sexually and/or romantically attracted to

- ○ Your desires, thoughts, fantasies, and sexual preferences

- ○ Your values, attitudes, and ideals about life, love, and sexual relationships

- ○ Your sexual behaviors — including masturbation

Objectives of Sex Education

- ○ Provide comprehensive good-quality information about sexual health and rights

- ○ Aware youth about risks they face and their vulnerability to the adverse consequences of sexual activity

- ○ Recognition of sexual orientation and gender identity

- ○ Impart knowledge of infections with human immunodeficiency virus (HIV), sexually transmitted infections (STIs) and reproductive tract infections (RTIs) and their adverse outcomes

- ○ Prevent unintended pregnancy and abortion

- ○ Provide guidance on sexual dysfunction and infertility

- ○ Spread awareness on sexual violence and harmful sexual practices

- ○ Promotion of safe and satisfying sexual experiences

Common Concerns About Provision of Sex Education

- *Sex education leads to early sex*: Research from around the world clearly indicates that sexuality education rarely, if ever, leads to early sexual initiation. Sexuality education can lead to later and more responsible sexual behaviour or may have no discernible impact on sexual behaviour.

- *Sex education deprives children of their 'innocence'*: In the absence of right information that is scientifically accurate, non-judgmental and age-appropriate, children and young people will often receive conflicting and sometimes damaging messages from their peers, the media or other sources. Sex education balances this through the provision of correct information and an emphasis on values and relationships.

- *Sex education is against our culture or religion*: Stakeholders in sex education should ensure cultural relevance and local adaptations, through engaging and building support among the custodians of culture in a given community.

- *It is the role of parents to educate young people about sexuality*: Sexuality education recognises the primary role of parents and the family as a source of information however, governments, schools, community must take responsibility to provide safe and supportive learning environment and the tools and materials to deliver good quality sex education.

- *Sex education may be good for young people, but not for young children*: Sexuality education encompasses a range of relationships, not only sexual relationships. Children are aware of and recognise these relationships long before they act on their sexuality and therefore need the skills to understand their bodies, relationships and feelings from an early age. These can then be built upon gradually, in line with the age and development of a child.

- *Sex education is already covered in other subjects (biology, life skills or civics education)*: Sex education encompasses a range of relationships, not only sexual relationships. Teachers should be encouraged to specialise in sexuality education through added emphasis on formalising the subject in the curriculum, as well as stronger professional development and support.

■ Sexual Activity Has Consequences: Examples From Uganda

It is important to recognise that sexual intercourse has consequences that go beyond unintended pregnancy or exposure to STIs including HIV, as illustrated in the case of Uganda:

'Ugandan boys and girls who have sex early are twice as likely not to complete secondary school as adolescents who have never had sex.' For many reasons, 'currently only 10% of boys and 8% of girls complete secondary school in Uganda' (Demographic and Health Survey Uganda, 2006).

In Uganda, thousands of boys are in jail for consensual sex with girls aged less than 18 years. Parents of many more have had to sell land and livestock to keep their sons out of jail. Pregnancy for a 17 year old Ugandan girl may mean that she has to leave school forever or marry a man with other wives (17% are in polygamous unions). About 50% of adolescent girls in Uganda give birth attended only by a relative or traditional birth attendant or alone.

2   Adolescent Sexual Behaviour

Adolescence is the most critical phase of life as changes in body is relatively fast and sexual desire begins to appear. Teens need complete and accurate information about sexuality to take good decisions about their sex life and relationships. Sex is generally associated with various risks including unwanted pregnancy and transmission of sexually transmitted diseases including HIV/AIDS.

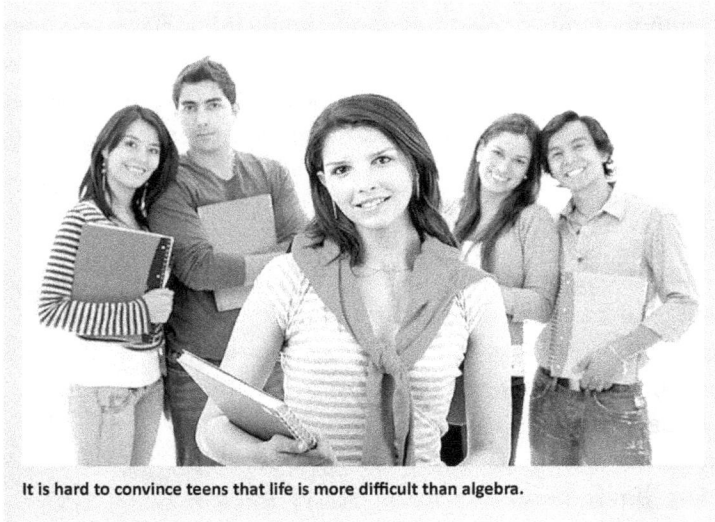

It is hard to convince teens that life is more difficult than algebra.

In case of adolescents, risks are elevated because their brains are not matured enough for right decisions. For teenage mothers, risks are associated more with socioeconomic factors than with the biological effects of age. Therefore, this is high time for parental involvement to guide young people so that they can take responsibility for their sexual and reproductive health. Knowing how to identify and respond to sexual behaviours in adolescents helps adults to support the development of healthy sexuality and protect young people from harm or abuse.

Quick Facts

- In 1900, most girls reached the puberty when they were 15 years old. In 1990s, the girls who had puberty were in the age of 12.
- In boys, testicles produce one million sperm per minute, 24 hours/day!
- There were 214,750 abortions in 2002 in the United States among 15–19 years old.

Body Image and Self-Esteem

Most of us want to make a good impression and care about how we look. Most girls are conscious about their looks and changes in body shape during puberty. Each adolescent makes a unique image about his/her body and most of the time body image is related to self-esteem of the individual. Some people struggle with their self-esteem and body image when they begin puberty. People with high self-esteem know themselves well. They are realistic and find friends that like and appreciate them for their qualities. However, many teenagers feel less confident about their looks and greatly influenced by comments of friends and relatives. They start comparing themselves with more attractive friends. People may also experience negative comments and hurtful teasing about the way they look from classmates and peers. Although these often come from ignorance, sometimes they can affect body image and self-esteem.

Puberty Period

Puberty is a period when you start making the change from being a child to being an adult. Signs of puberty include growing breasts, pimples, body hair and changes in emotions. Puberty in girls usually starts between the ages of 8 and 13 and ends by around 14. For boys, puberty usually starts between 10 and 14, and ends by around 15 or 16. During puberty, menstruation begins in girls while boys' sex organs start forming sperm cells. During puberty, you will likely see new hair growing in your pubic area, under your

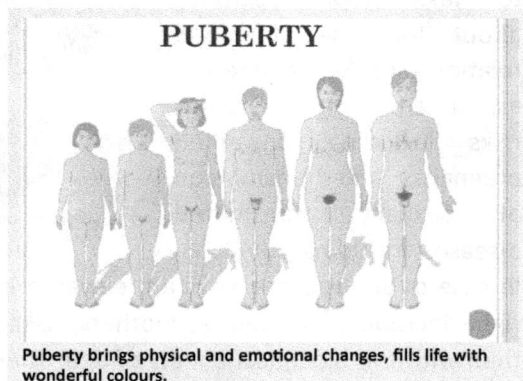

PUBERTY

Puberty brings physical and emotional changes, fills life with wonderful colours.

arms, and on your legs. Puberty not only brings changes in physical appearance but also in thoughts and emotions. Teens are now able to understand more complex problems, they can understand their likes and dislikes and choose friend of their choice. They may develop strong and deep emotions and plan their future. Puberty can spark some brand-new urges, and you may start having strong feelings for someone you like. You may start thinking more about your sexuality.

The only test of the development of intellect is whether one has started controlling uncontrolled desires.
—*Sriram Sharma Acharya*

Building Healthy Relationship

Friends, classmates, colleagues often spend lots of time in study or fun activities. During this period, a boy or a girl may get attracted to each other and enter into dating relationship. Relationships can provide you with great happiness, but they can also be very challenging. It's important to know that relationships can be complicated, unhealthy, or even unsafe. Understanding the truth about unhealthy relationships can help you decide course of mutual

True relationship is based on mutual trust, respect and commitment.

relationship. Unfortunately, too many teenagers are in relationships that involve a loss of sexual and reproductive control. Knowing what this looks like can help you identify when something is not right in your relationship. Remember! communication, trust, and respect are key to healthy relationships. Healthy relationships make you feel good about who YOU are and SAFE with the other person.

Significance of 'Safe Sex'

Sexual intercourse causes exchange of body's internal fluids between partners, it is important to realize significance of safe sex practices. If you are aware of the following facts, you can save yourself and your partner from health hazards. Here are few tips:

o   Choose low risk sexual activities such as kissing, hugging, masturbation etc.

o   The best way of safe sex is making sexual relations with one partner who has no sexually transmitted infections.

o   Use condoms during vaginal or anal intercourse

o   Avoid oral sex with the partner without condom

o   Avoid drinks and drug before any sexual activity

o   Keep genital area clean and avoid tight clothing

o   Choose minimum and trusted sex partner

o   Ensure medical check-up of both partners for STIs before sexual intercourse

How Parents Can Provide Sex Education to Children

Parents need to be able to address the physical and behavioural aspects of human sexuality with their children, and children need to be informed and equipped with the knowledge and skills to make responsible decisions about sexuality, relationships, HIV and other sexually transmitted infections. Parents can take the clue from the following points to educate kids on sexuality and related issues.

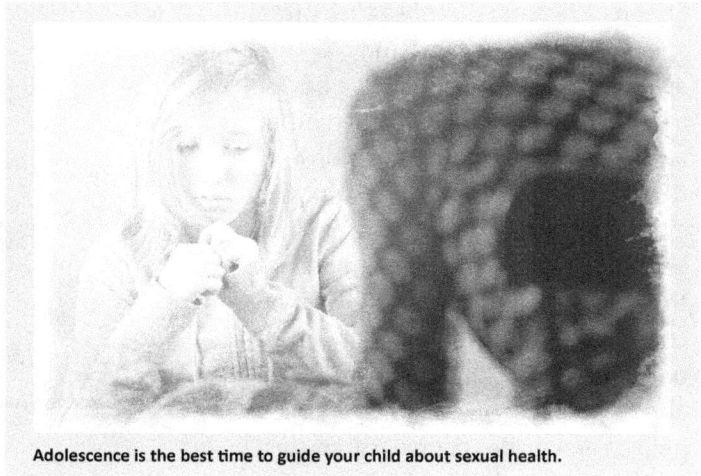

Adolescence is the best time to guide your child about sexual health.

○ Use pictorial books to help in easy learning of sex-related topics.

○ Provide basic knowledge about sex organs and ask them not to touch their friends below waist.

○ Teach children about sex hygiene and how to clean genital organs to avoid infection.

○ Documentaries, teaching videos available on Internet can be showed to children.

○ Invite known kids at home and discuss various topics one-by-one starting from 'Know Your Body'. Demarcate the discussion in terms of unhealthy gossips. Make it a part of learning process.

○ Discuss sexual health topics such as need of nutritious food and prevention of sexual diseases through examples.

○ Educate kids about right and wrong behaviour in interaction with opposite sex in school or locality.

○ Tell your ward how to tackle sexual abuse or any kind of discrimination on basis of his/her gender.

○ Warn against access of sexual contents from Internet, CD, magazines or mobile.

○ If you find child engaged in some unethical sex practices or pornography, instead of scolding him discuss sex-related issues and resolve queries with positive approach.

Why Waiting for Sexual Relationship Makes Sense

As people pass from childhood through the teen years, bodies develop and change. Teens experience a new phenomenon of sexual attraction. For some, sexual feelings and thoughts can be intense while for others it may be confusing. Emergence of romantic feeling during puberty is quite normal but due to lack of information about handling the sexual behaviour often creates problems in personal life. Some

Hormones arouse sexual urge but abstinence is best way to gain partner's trust.

try to experiment with sexual experiences with friends or colleagues without knowing consequences. Having sex before your body and mind attain maturity can seriously hurt your relationship and your feelings. You could wind up with an unplanned pregnancy or catch sexually transmitted disease (STDs). Most serious consequence of unsafe sex is pregnancy and teenage is not appropriate time for getting pregnant. Sexuality is not fun or means of enjoyment. It is a responsibility that prepares your mind and body to attain maturity and establish long term relationship with life partner.

Abstinence is the only 100 percent effective method for avoiding unintended pregnancy and sexually transmitted infections, including HIV. Teens—especially young teens—should be encouraged to delay sexual initiation. Educators should acknowledge the importance of abstinence and provide youth with the knowledge, attitudes, and skills necessary to make abstinence work. Experts say complete abstinence—not having vaginal, oral, and anal sex—is safest. Avoiding intimate sexual contact, including skin-to-skin genital contact, is the only sure way to prevent all STDs and pregnancy.

Reproductive system is an integration of internal and external sex organs of an organism which work together to create new life. Unlike most of the organs of human body, the organs of male reproductive system differ with female. Fluids, hormones, and pheromones in the body are also important accessories to the reproductive system. The reproductive system facilitate transfer of genetic material from male and female to offspring that eventually builds physical and behavioral traits. Sexual reproduction offers the benefit of generating genetic variation among offspring. Male's role in sexual reproduction is ejaculation of sperm into female's vagina leading to fertilization of egg. Female sex organs take all the responsibility to nourish, develop and give birth to baby in about nine months.

Female Reproductive System

Female reproductive system has muscular elastic bag like structure called uterus and pair of ovaries attached to it on either sides. Two tube-like structures emerge out of uterus on either side. These are called oviducts. Uterus opens into vagina through narrow cervical canal. The vagina is attached to the uterus through the cervix, while the uterus is attached to the ovaries via the fallopian tubes. The cervix is flexible so it

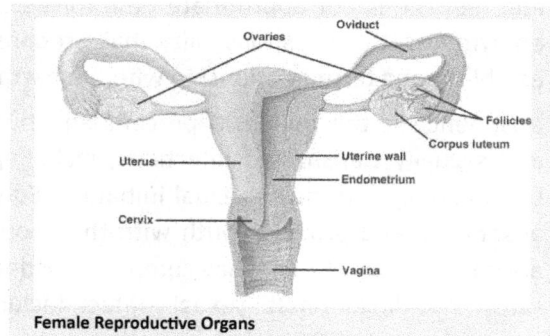

Female Reproductive Organs

can expand to let a child pass through childbirth. The vagina meets the outside at the vulva, which also includes the labia, clitoris and urethra. Each ovary contains hundreds of egg cells or ova which take part in the process of fertilization. The hymen covers the opening of the vagina. It is a thin piece of tissue and may be stretched or torn during first sexual intercourse or tampon. If it does tear, it may bleed a little bit.

The breasts are also an important part of the reproductive system. After a woman gives birth, her breasts make milk to feed the baby. The milk is made in the cells of the lobules inside the breast and travels through ducts to the nipple used for child feeding.

Male Reproductive System

The organs and structures of the male reproductive system give men the ability to fertilise a woman's ovum (egg) to produce a baby. The male reproductive system consists of organs responsible for production, storage and ejaculation of sperm. Production takes place in a pair of testes, which are housed in the scrotum that provides proper temperature for formation of sperm cells. Immature sperm then travel to the epididymis for further development and storage. Leading from the epididymis is the vas deferens. The vas deferens carries sperm to the penis. In between, three accessory glands provide fluids that lubricate the duct system and nourish the sperm cells. They are the seminal vesicles, the prostate gland, and the Cowper glands. The mixture of sperm, fluid from the prostate and fluid from the seminal vesicles is called semen.

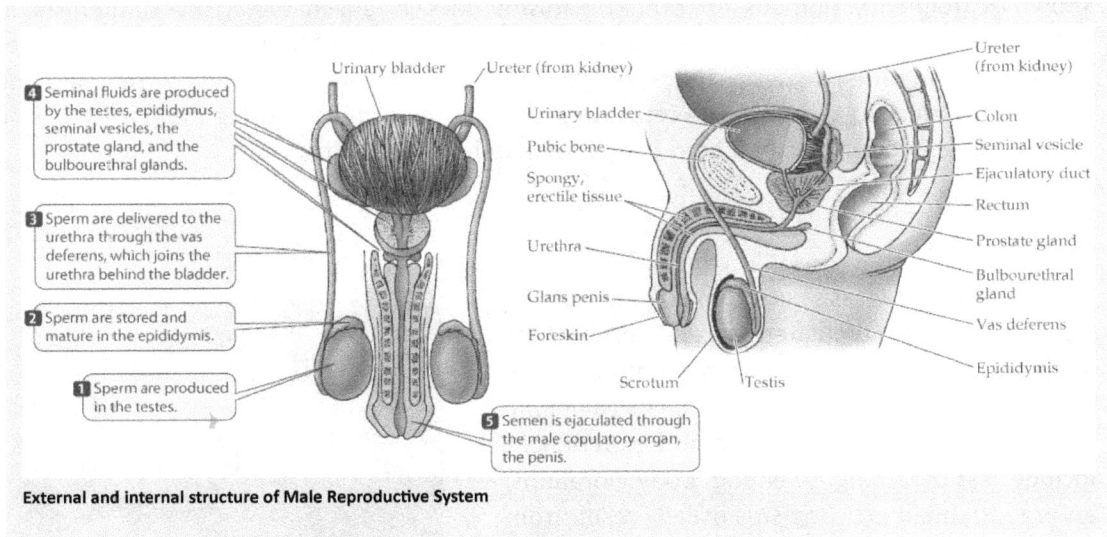

4 Seminal fluids are produced by the testes, epididymus, seminal vesicles, the prostate gland, and the bulbourethral glands.

3 Sperm are delivered to the urethra through the vas deferens, which joins the urethra behind the bladder.

2 Sperm are stored and mature in the epididymis.

1 Sperm are produced in the testes.

5 Semen is ejaculated through the male copulatory organ, the penis.

Urinary bladder   Ureter (from kidney)   Ureter (from kidney)   Colon   Seminal vesicle   Ejaculatory duct   Rectum   Prostate gland   Bulbourethral gland   Vas deferens   Epididymis

Urinary bladder   Pubic bone   Spongy, erectile tissue   Urethra   Glans penis   Foreskin   Scrotum   Testis

External and internal structure of Male Reproductive System

When sexually aroused, a number of changes occur inside the penis. The arteries supplying the penis expand allowing more blood to enter its tissues. The increase in blood flow causes the penis to enlarge. This is called erection, which results in increase of penis size by 2–3 times. On reaching orgasm, the contraction of muscles causes a reflex action which means it is not consciously controlled. This process is called ejaculation through which male deposits sperm into female vagina. The volume of semen in a typical ejaculation is between 2.5–5 millilitres (mL) with more than 20 million sperm per mL.

Process of Sexual Reproduction

In the reproductive process, two kinds of sex cells, or gametes, are involved, the male gamete, or sperm, and the female gamete, the egg or ovum. The process of sexual reproduction involves internal fertilization (union) by sexual intercourse. During this process, the male inserts his penis into the female's vagina and ejaculates semen, which contains sperm. The sperm then travels through the vagina and cervix into the uterus or fallopian tubes

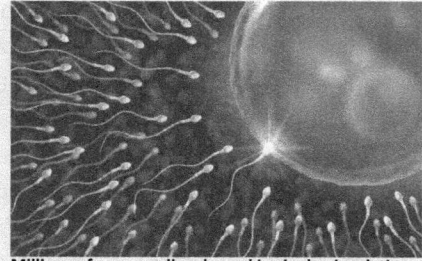
Millions of sperm cells released in single ejaculation; Only one fertilizes egg.

leading to fertilization of the ovum. Upon successful fertilization and implantation, gestation of the fetus then occurs within the female's uterus for approximately nine months, this process is known as pregnancy. Humans, like other organisms, pass certain characteristics of themselves to the next generation through their genes, the special carriers of human traits. These genes come from the father's sperm and the mother's egg, which are produced by the male and female reproductive systems. The fetus undergoes many changes during pregnancy period and develops into full matured baby in approximately nine months.

Orgasm

Orgasm, also known as sexual climax, is the sudden discharge of accumulated sexual excitement achieved through series of rhythmic contractions of muscles in pelvic region. Each person has a unique experience of orgasm but common experiences include fast breathing, sweating, body vibrations, an urge to moan etc. Orgasms usually result from physical sexual stimulation of the penis in males and the clitoris in females. It can be achieved by masturbation, penetrative or non-penetrative

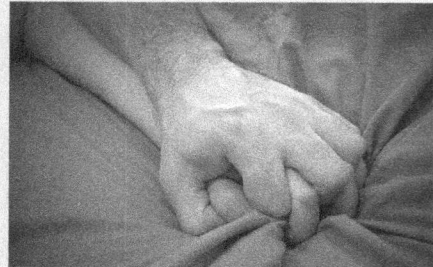
Orgasm is healthy for body and mind as it relieves stress.

sex with the partner. The orgasm is often a relaxing experience attributed to the release of the neurohormones oxytocin and prolactin, as well as endorphins into the blood which provide pleasure and satisfaction. During orgasm, the sensations in both sexes are extremely pleasurable and are often felt throughout the body. In addition to physical stimulation, orgasm can be achieved from psychological arousal alone, such as during dreaming or nocturnal emission.

Menstruation Cycle

Menstruation is a woman's monthly bleeding in which blood flows from uterus and passes out of body through vagina. Most menstrual periods last from 3 to 5 days. But anywhere between 2–7 days is normal. Having regular menstrual cycle is a sign that important parts of your body is working properly. The average menstrual cycle is 28 days long.

A menstrual cycle is counted from the first day of 1 period to the first day of the next period. The rise and fall of hormones

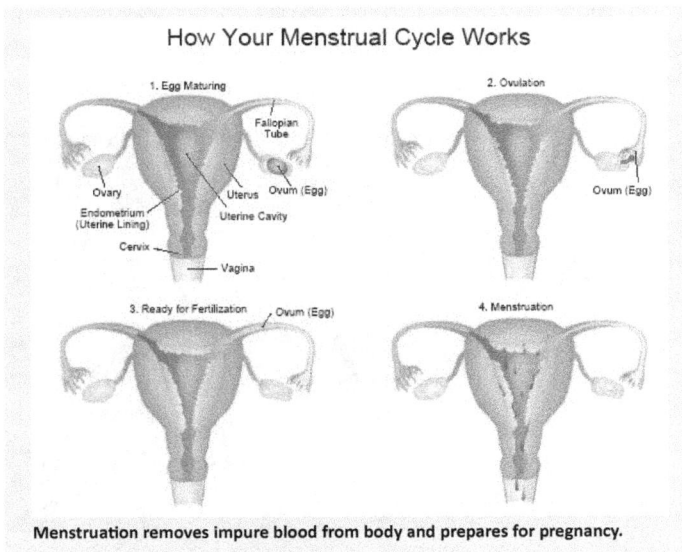

How Your Menstrual Cycle Works

Menstruation removes impure blood from body and prepares for pregnancy.

during the month control the menstrual cycle. In the first half of the cycle, levels of estrogen start to rise. Estrogen also makes the lining of the uterus grow and thicken. As the lining of the uterus is growing, an egg or ovum in one of the ovaries starts to mature. The lining is rich in blood and nutrients. At about day of 14 of an average 28-day cycle, the egg leaves the ovary. This is called ovulation. Over the next few days, the egg travels down the fallopian tube towards the uterus. If a sperm unites with the egg, it fertilizes to form zygote. A woman becomes pregnant if the egg is fertilized by a man's sperm cell and attaches to the uterine wall. After fertilization, women do not undergo menstruation until child birth. If the egg is not fertilized, hormone levels will drop around day 25 and the egg will break apart shedding lining of uterus. Thus the next menstrual cycle begins with the discharge of blood along with unfertilized egg.

Usually, girls get her first period at the age of 12. But any variation between ages of 8 and 15 is normal. Women usually have periods until age of 50 after which she is unable to produce eggs or get pregnant. This is called menopause. Like menstruation, menopause can vary from women to women and may occur between ages of 45 and 55.

Primary signs of menstruation:

(a) Abdominal cramping; (b) Lower back pain; (c) Mood swings or irritability

(d) Headache and fatigue; (e) Food cravings

Sex Determination

In humans and many other animal species, sex is determined by specific chromosomes. The event of sex determinations occurs during union of male's sperm with female egg. The female has two X chromosomes (XX) and the male an X and Y (XY).

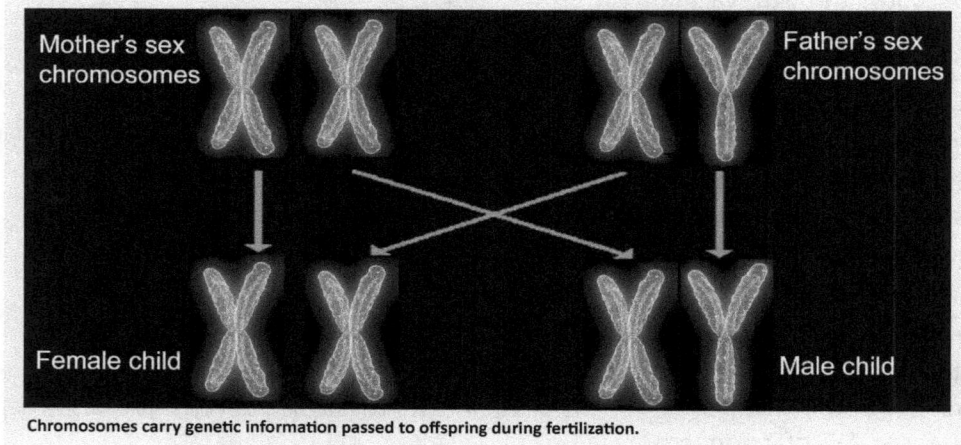

Chromosomes carry genetic information passed to offspring during fertilization.

During the process of meiosis when the sex cell division takes place in adults (dividing to 23 chromosomes), the female cell will divide into two X sex cells. The male cell divides into an X and Y cell. A person has 46 chromosomes in total; 23 chromosomes come from the mother and 23 from the father.

Therefore, all ova (plural for ovum) from the female contain only X chromosome. In a male during meiosis, the cells are split up in two as well. So some sperm cells contain an X chromosome and others Y chromosomes.

During fertilisation an X sperm cell in combination with a female X cell makes a girl (XX). If a Y sperm cell joins with an ovum, a boy is produced (XY). Therefore, 23 chromosomes from either parent gives the child the total number of 46 chromosomes. The Y chromosome induces testis formation and thus male sexual development; in the absence of a Y chromosome, gonads differentiate into ovaries and female development ensues.

Quick Facts

- The ovum must be fertilized within 12–24 hours. It takes 10 hours for a sperm to fertilize an egg.
- Sperm can survive 4–5 days inside a woman's body.

Sex can be great but it can also carry risks, such as unwanted pregnancy and transmission of sexually transmitted infections (STIs). A woman can get pregnant if a man's sperm reaches one of her eggs (ova). Contraception tries to stop this happening by keeping the egg and sperm apart or by stopping egg production. Thus contraception or birth control, are methods or devices used to prevent pregnancy. Planning, provision and use of birth control is called family planning. The best way to reduce the risk of unintended pregnancy among women who are sexually active is to use effective birth control correctly and consistently. Which method works best for you depend on a number of factors, including your age, medical and family history, and any medication you are taking. If you are trying to choose a method, learning about each of them may help you make your decision.

Less birth control *More self-control*

Importance of Contraception

Contraceptive use in developing countries is estimated to have decreased the number of maternal deaths by 40%. Globally, as of 2009, approximately 60% of those who are married and able to have children use birth control. Birth control also improves child survival by lengthening the time between pregnancies. Teenage pregnancies, especially among younger teens, are at greater risk of adverse outcomes including early birth, low birth weight, and death of the infant. In the United States, 82% of pregnancies in those between 15 and 19 are unplanned. Comprehensive sex education and access to birth control are effective in decreasing pregnancy rates in this age group. In the developing world women's earnings, assets, weight, and their children's schooling and health all improve with greater access to birth control. Birth control increases economic growth because of fewer dependent children, more women participating in the workforce, and less consumption of scarce resources.

Popular Methods of Contraception

Temporary Methods:

1 Condom: Condom is a thin sheath, usually made of latex or polyurethane worn on external genital organ during sexual intercourse as protection from unwanted pregnancy or sexually transmitted diseases. Condom is most common and effective method of birth control. There are two types of condoms: male condom and female condom. Male condoms are worn on penis while female condoms are inserted into vagina before sexual intercourse. Condoms act as barrier between

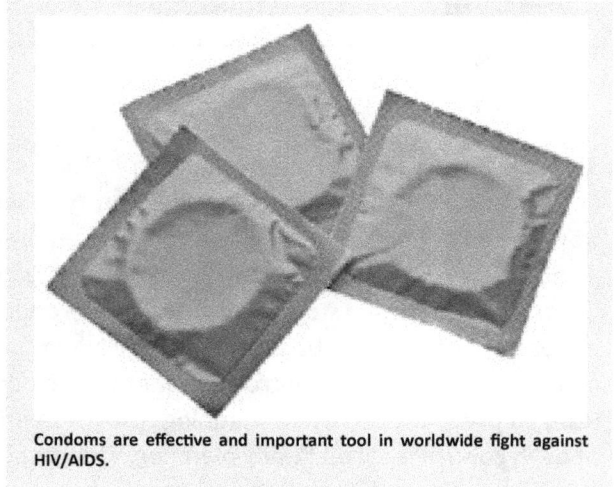

Condoms are effective and important tool in worldwide fight against HIV/AIDS.

male and female sex organs in which ejaculation takes place and keep sperm from entering the vagina preventing fertilization of egg. Effectiveness of condom depends on quality and correct use during sex. If it breaks during sex, woman must use emergency contraception (morning after pills) to avoid pregnancy. The condom should be put on before any genital contact. Sperm may come out of the penis before the male ejaculates, so put the condom on before any skin-to-skin contact begins.

How to Properly Put on a Male Condom

○ Check the expiration date on the condom

○ Carefully open the package so that it may not get damaged

○ Put the rolled-up condom over the tip of your penis

○ Have sex!

○ After ejaculation carefully hold onto the condom at the base of your penis as you pull it out, to make sure it does not slip off.

○ Throw it in dustbin. Do not flush your condoms down the toilet.

2. **Birth Control Pills:** Birth control pills are a kind of oral contraception that women can take daily to prevent pregnancy. Most of the pills contain artificial versions of the female hormones estrogen and progesterone, which women produce naturally in their ovaries. The hormones in the pill work by keeping eggs from leaving the ovaries and making cervical mucus thicker preventing sperms from joining the egg. When taken correctly, the pill is over 99% effective at preventing pregnancy. You need to take the pill every day at the same time for 21 days, then stop for seven days, and during this week you have a period-type bleed. Then start taking the pill again after seven days.

3. **IUDs Device:** IUD stands for 'Intrauterine Device'. IUDs are small, "T-shaped" devices made of flexible plastic and copper device that are implanted in woman's uterus to prevent pregnancy. The IUD works by stopping the sperm and egg from surviving in the womb or fallopian tubes. An IUD works as soon as it's put in, and lasts for five to 10 years. IUD may not suite every woman and few may complain of bleeding and pain. In that case, she could use

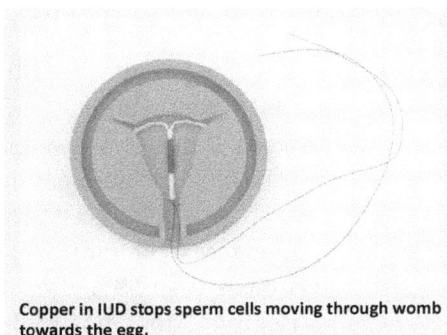

Copper in IUD stops sperm cells moving through womb towards the egg.

other contraceptive method. IUD does not protect against sexually transmitted infections (STIs).

4. **Contraceptive Patches:** The contraceptive patch is a thin, beige, plastic sticky patch that sticks to the skin once a week for three weeks in a row, followed by a patch-free week. It delivers hormones into female body through skin. It contains the same hormones as the combined pill, and it works in the same way. The patch is more than 99% effective at preventing pregnancy.

5. **Outercourse:** Outercourse is sexual stimulation without vaginal penetration. Outercourse is nearly 100 percent effective at preventing pregnancy. It allows a couple to be sexual, more intimate, and even orgasmic without any risk of pregnancy. It includes sexual acts such as masturbation, kissing, foreplay and sex talks.

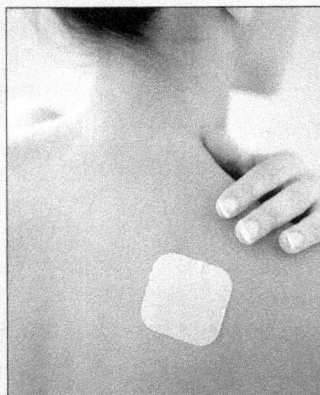

Contraceptive patch releases hormones to prevent pregnancy.

Outercourse can be used as safer sex to help prevent STDs if semen and vaginal fluids are not exchanged. However, in outercourse, it is difficult to abstain from intercourse during sexual act, which may lead to pregnancy or infection.

Permanent Methods

Male Sterilization: Male Sterilization or Vasectomy is a form of birth control method for men in which the tube carrying sperm is blocked to prevent pregnancy. Vasectomy is done if you do not want to have a child biologically in the future. Sperm are made in the testicles. They pass through two tubes called the vasa deferentia to other glands and mix with seminal fluids to form semen. Vasectomy prevents sperm from reaching the seminal fluid (semen), which is ejaculated from the penis during sex. In most cases, vasectomy is more than 99% effective. However, Vasectomy does not protect from STIs.

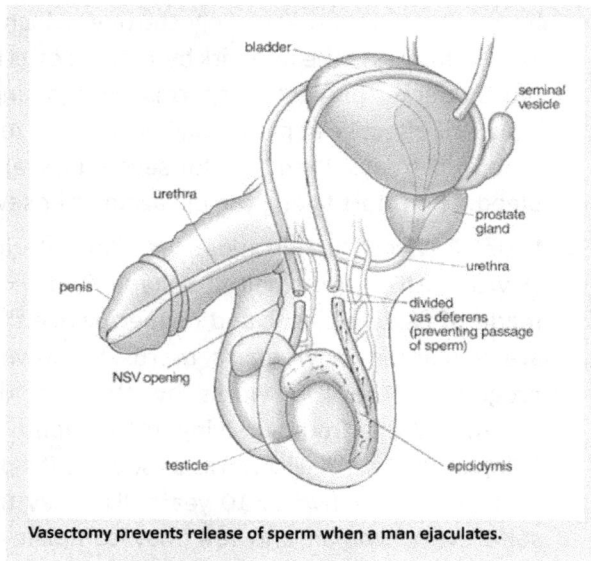

Vasectomy prevents release of sperm when a man ejaculates.

Female Sterilization: Female Sterilization is a form of birth control method for women. All sterilization procedures are meant to be permanent. Sterilization method does not change body hormones. During a sterilization procedure, a health care provider closes or blocks a woman's fallopian tubes. Eggs are made in a woman's ovaries. One egg is released each month. It passes through one of the fallopian tubes toward the uterus. Sterilization blocks each tube thus preventing fertilization of eggs. Sterilization is safe and, because it lasts for life, it is simple and convenient. It allows a woman to enjoy sex without worrying about pregnancy.

There are lots of things to consider when deciding which form of contraception is best for you. The following questions can help you decide which method is most suitable:
- Can you remember regular contraception every day?
- Do you feel comfortable in putting latex during sex?
- Do you need offspring in future i.e. wants temporary or permanent contraceptive methods?
- Do you feel comfortable inserting contraception devises into your body?
- Are you overweight?
- Do you smoke?
- Does hormonal contraceptive suits your body?

Love and sex are important aspect of life. But sexual activity can also be associated with risks and health problems. Unprotected sex may cause sexually transmitted infections or STIs and some are life threatening. Ignoring or self-treatment of such disease increases chance of complications. Many STIs spread internally and do show any symptom. Teenagers are most vulnerable to these infections as they are mostly unaware about causes and consequences of unsafe sex practices. With changes in lifestyle and ignorance towards STIs, deadly infections such as HIV, syphilis, gonorrhea and unintended pregnancies are prevalent in young people including teenagers.

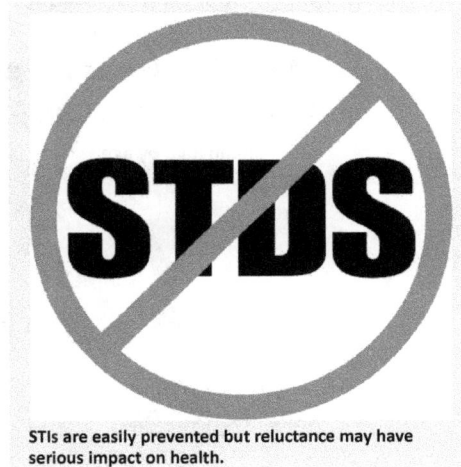

STIs are easily prevented but reluctance may have serious impact on health.

Sexually Transmitted Diseases

Sexually transmitted diseases or STDs are infections caused by unsafe sexual practices. Anyone who has sexual contact including oral sex, anal sex, and contact between genital areas can get an STD. STDs spread very easily, and young people have been hit hard by them. In fact, 1 out of 4 teenage girls have an STD. Sometimes people are too scared or embarrassed to ask for STD information or testing. But keep in mind that many STDs are easy to treat — and dangerous if they're not detected and treated. Untreated STDs can cause some scary health problems. These include problems with your reproductive system, pain, cancer, and permanent damage to your body. STDs often have no signs or symptoms (asymptomatic). Even with no symptoms, however, you can pass the infection to your sex partners. The surest way to avoid getting an STD is not to have sexual intercourse or other kinds of intimate sexual contact with unknown or infected person. It's also a good idea to stay away from drugs and alcohol, which can lead to having unsafe sex.

Common Sexually Transmitted Diseases and their Symptoms

a. **Chlamydia:** Chlamydia is a bacterial infection of your genital tract. Symptoms include painful urination, vaginal discharge pain during sexual intercourse in women, discharge from the penis in men.

b. **Gonorrhea:** Gonorrhea is a bacterial infection of your genital tract. Its symptoms are thick, cloudy or bloody discharge from the penis or vagina, heavy menstrual bleeding or bleeding between periods, painful, swollen testicles.

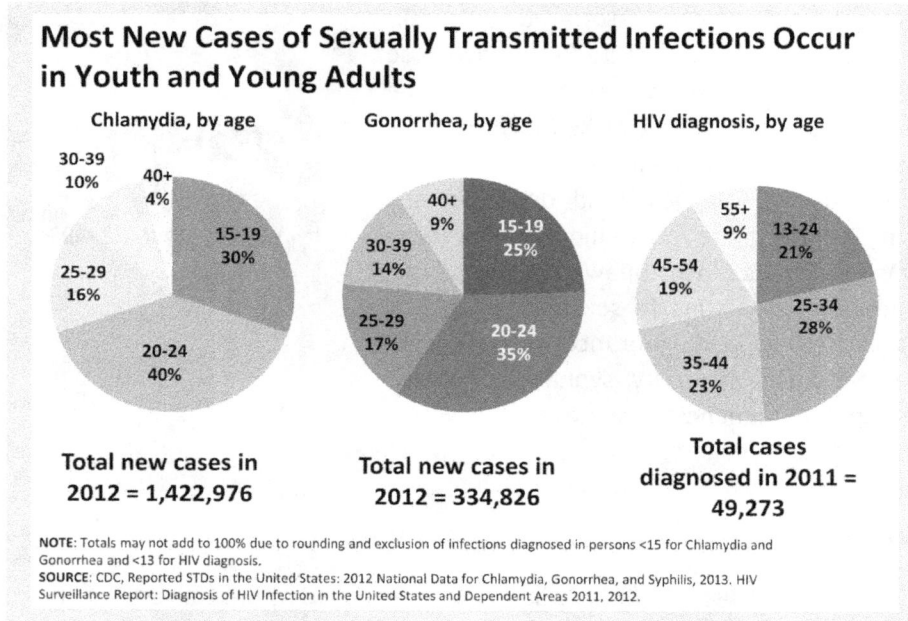

Most New Cases of Sexually Transmitted Infections Occur in Youth and Young Adults

Chlamydia, by age

30-39 10%
40+ 4%
15-19 30%
25-29 16%
20-24 40%

Total new cases in 2012 = 1,422,976

Gonorrhea, by age

40+ 9%
30-39 14%
15-19 25%
25-29 17%
20-24 35%

Total new cases in 2012 = 334,826

HIV diagnosis, by age

55+ 9%
13-24 21%
45-54 19%
25-34 28%
35-44 23%

Total cases diagnosed in 2011 = 49,273

NOTE: Totals may not add to 100% due to rounding and exclusion of infections diagnosed in persons <15 for Chlamydia and Gonorrhea and <13 for HIV diagnosis.
SOURCE: CDC, Reported STDs in the United States: 2012 National Data for Chlamydia, Gonorrhea, and Syphilis, 2013. HIV Surveillance Report: Diagnosis of HIV Infection in the United States and Dependent Areas 2011, 2012.

c. **Trichomoniasis:** Trichomoniasis is a common STI caused by parasite called Trichomonas vaginalis. Common symptoms of this disease include clear, white, greenish or yellowish vaginal discharge in women, discharge from penis in men, itching or irritation in vagina and penis, pain during sexual intercourse.

d. **HIV:** HIV is an infection with the human immunodeficiency virus. It can lead to AIDS, a chronic, life-threatening disease. Within a month or two of HIV entering the body, 40% to 90% of people experience flu-like symptoms. However, it may not show any symptom for several years after entering the body. Symptoms of HIV infection are swollen lymph nodes, diarrhea, weight loss, fever, cough and shortness of breath, persistent, unexplained fatigue, unusual, opportunistic infections.

e. **Genital herpes:** Highly contagious, genital herpes is caused by a type of the herpes simplex virus (HSV). Common symptoms are small red bumps, blisters (vesicles) or open sores (ulcers) in the genital, anal and nearby areas, pain or itching around the genital area, buttocks and inner thighs.

f. **Human papillomavirus (HPV) infection:** HPV infection occurs when the virus enters the body through a cut or abrasion in the outer layer of skin. HPV is recognised by small, flesh-colored or gray swellings in the genital area, several warts close together that take on a cauliflower shape, itching or discomfort in genital area.

g. **Hepatitis:** Hepatitis A, hepatitis B and hepatitis C are all contagious viral infections that affect your liver. Symptoms are fatigue, nausea and vomiting, abdominal pain or discomfort, loss of appetite, and fever.

h. **Syphilis:** Syphilis is a bacterial infection. The disease affects your genitals, skin and mucous membranes. The signs and symptoms of syphilis vary depending in which of the four stages it presents (primary, secondary, latent, and tertiary). The primary stage classically presents with a single chancre (a firm, painless, non-itchy skin ulceration), secondary syphilis with a diffuse rash which frequently involves the palms of the hands and soles of the feet, latent syphilis with little to no symptoms, and tertiary syphilis with gummas, neurological, or cardiac symptoms.

When to See Doctor

○ You have ever had sex (vaginal, oral, or anal) or intimate sexual contact

○ It has been three months or more since your last period and you haven't gotten it again

○ You have stomach pain, fever, and fluid coming from your vagina that is yellow, gray, or green with a strong smell

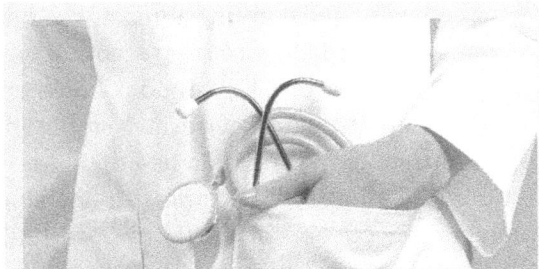

Stick to safe sex practices and seek doctor's advice on sexual health problems.

○ You are having problems with your period, like a lot of pain, bleeding heavily, or bleeding for longer than usual, or it has stopped coming regularly

○ You have not gotten your period by the age of 15 or within three years of when your breasts started to grow

○ You are having sex and missed your period

Women's Sexual Health Problems

Vaginal Infections: Normal vaginal discharge is beneficial and serves several purposes: cleaning and moistening the vagina, and helping to prevent and fight infections. Vaginal fluids should be clear, white, or off-white in color. However any change in odor, colour, and texture indicates vaginal infection. Signs that you may have a vaginal infection include itching, burning, pain in or around your vagina, or a problem with your vaginal discharge (fluid). Sometimes, excess discharge or dryness of vagina occurs. Vaginal infection may indicate STDs but not all infections are caused by sexual contact. To avoid vaginal infections:

❍ Keep your genital area clean

❍ Change your underwear every day

❍ Avoid unsafe sexual contact

❍ Drink enough liquids

❍ Abstinence is the safest way to avoid infections

Dysfunctional Uterine Bleeding: Dysfunctional uterine bleeding (DUB) is irregular uterine bleeding that occurs due to changes in hormone levels. Dysfunctional uterine bleeding (DUB) occurs most often before age 20 and after age 40. Compared with typical menses, bleeding may occur more frequently, involve more blood loss (> 7 days or > 80 mL) during menses or occur frequently and irregularly between menses. Treatment involves hormone therapy, such as oral contraceptives, or with NSAIDs (Nonsteroidal anti-inflammatory drug).

Unwanted Pregnancy: Unwanted or unintended pregnancies are pregnancies that are mistimed, unplanned or unwanted at the time of conception occur due to sexual intercourse without using or failure of contraception methods. Available contraception methods include use of birth control pills, condom (male or female), contraceptive implant, contraceptive injection, intrauterine device and sterilization. Unintended pregnancy has been linked to numerous maternal and child health problems. Unintended pregnancies are the main reason for induced abortions. According to one study, over one-third of living people in the United States under 31 years of age (born since 1982) were the result of unintended pregnancies.

Breast Cancer: Breast cancer is type of cancer that develops from breast tissue. Signs of breast cancer may include a lump in the breast, a change in breast shape, dimpling of the skin, swelling in the armpit, pain or tenderness in the breast, or a red scaly patch of skin. Risk factors for developing breast cancer include late or early child, genetic factors, obesity, hormone replacement therapy, etc. The diagnosis of breast cancer is confirmed by taking a biopsy. Women who are diagnosed with breast cancer before age 40 have slightly poorer rate of survival. More than 9 out of 10 women who detect breast cancer early live at least five years — and many live much longer.

How Do People Get AIDS

AIDS (Acquired immunodeficiency syndrome) is a syndrome caused by a virus called HIV (Human Immunodeficiency Virus). HIV is found in the body fluids of an infected person (semen and vaginal fluids, blood and breast milk). It kills or damages the body's immune system cells. The virus is passed from one person to another through blood-to-blood and sexual contact. In addition, infected pregnant women can pass HIV to their babies during pregnancy, delivering the baby during childbirth, and through breast feeding. HIV can be transmitted in many ways, such as unprotected vaginal, oral sex, anal sex, blood transfusion, and contaminated needles. The first signs of HIV infection may be swollen glands and flu-like symptoms. Severe symptoms may not appear until months or years

Main symptoms of
AIDS

Neurological
- Encephalitis
- Meningitis

Eyes
- Retinitis

Lungs
- Pneumocystis pneumonia
- Tuberculosis (multiple organs)
- Tumors

Skin
- Tumors

Gastrointestinal
- Esophagitis
- Chronic diarrhea
- Tumors

A person is diagnosed with AIDS when immune system becomes too weak to fight infections.

later. An HIV test confirms diagnosis. Medications may suppress the virus and delay the onset of AIDS.

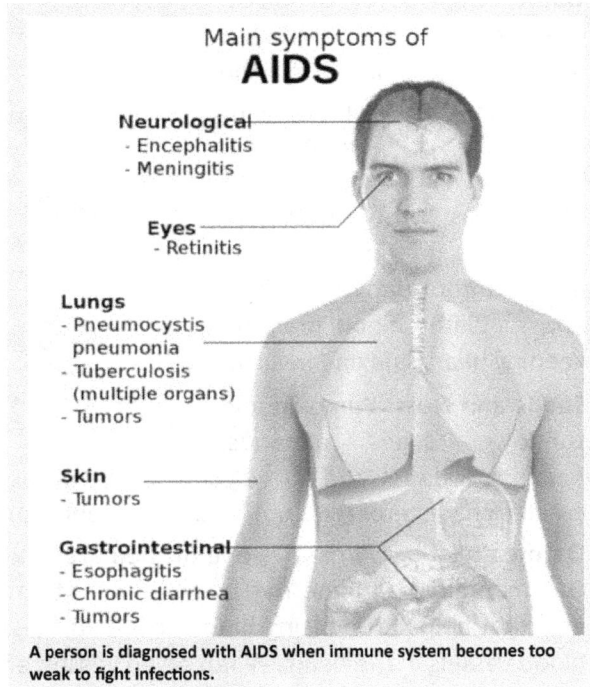

There are several steps you can take to protect yourself against HIV/AIDS and other STDs:

- Use a new condom every time you have sex
- Always use new or sterilized needle for injection
- If you are pregnant, test for HIV infection
- If you have any sign or symptom of AIDS, immediately seek medical assistance
- HIV positive mothers should not nurse a child
- The fewer sex partners you have, the more you reduce your risk of HIV infection

As the infection progresses, it interferes more and more with the immune system, making the person much more susceptible to common infections. Therefore, people with AIDS are at higher risk of various diseases. There is no cure or vaccine for AIDS. Without treatment, the average survival time after infection with HIV is estimated to be 9 to 11 years.

Food That Improves Sexual Health

Garlic: High level of allicin present in garlic increases direct blood flow to the sexual organs. Allicin contains Manganese, Vitamin B6, Vitamin C and trace amounts of various other nutrients. Garlic has anti-inflammatory and anti-oxidative effects and regulates blood pressure keeping heart safe and healthy.

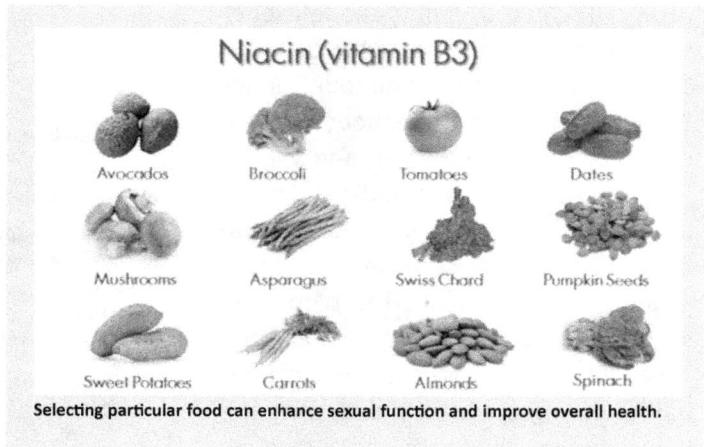

Niacin (vitamin B3)

Avocados, Broccoli, Tomatoes, Dates, Mushrooms, Asparagus, Swiss Chard, Pumpkin Seeds, Sweet Potatoes, Carrots, Almonds, Spinach

Selecting particular food can enhance sexual function and improve overall health.

Seeds and Nuts: Pumpkin and sunflower seeds, almonds, peanuts, walnuts, and nuts all contain the necessary monounsaturated fats with which body creates cholesterol required by sex hormones for proper functioning.

Oatmeal: Eating oatmeal is one of the natural ways to boost testosterone level in the body. Oats contain L-arginine has been used to treat erectile dysfunction. L-arginine, an amino acid that helps in reducing blood vessel stiffness. Like Viagra, it helps relax muscles around blood vessels in the penis. When blood vessels are dilated, blood flow increases so a man can maintain an erection.

Avocado: Avocado is rich in folic acid, potassium and vitamin B6 and enhances body's sexual energy. They are rich in unsaturated fats and low in saturated fat, making them good for your heart. Strong heart means good supply of blood in arteries and high sex drive.

Dark chocolate: The antioxidant in dark chocolate enhances libido in both men and women. Dark chocolate contains a compound called phenylethylamine that releases the same endorphins triggered by sexual activities. Experts believe that in order to get health benefit try dark chocolate with 70 percent cacao.

Bananas: Bananas are a great source of B-group vitamins and potassium, both used in sex hormone production. Eating banana in raw form retains essential nutrients.

Maca: Maca plays significant role in alleviating impotency. It increases level of testosterone and sperm count in men. At the same time it balances your hormones and increases fertility.

Strawberries: Eating strawberries and raspberries can increase your sex drive as these fruits are rich in Zinc which governs testosterone. They are also incredibly high in anti-oxidants which helps to optimise blood flow to the sex organs.

28

Masturbation

Masturbation is the self-stimulation of the genitals to achieve sexual pleasure and orgasm. Reading or viewing pornography, sexual fantasy, or other erotic stimuli may lead to a desire for masturbation. Moderate masturbation has no adverse effects on your body. It relieves stress and provides sexual satisfaction without harming others. Masturbation saves from immoral sexual behavior and pre-marital sex. However, excessive masturbation creates a problem when one reaches a point where he does not have any sperms to ejaculate. There are many harmful myths about masturbation that may cause us to feel uncomfortable about it. So, do not panic. Do not feel guilt or punish yourself. Just try to overcome the habit of masturbation so that it remains in your control and you maintain a sound health.

- It is essential that a firm commitment be made to control the habit.
- Do not believe the myths about the harms of masturbation. Masturbation will not cause infertility, premature ejaculation, or impotence.
- Stop touching your private parts frequently. Block porn websites and destroy all collections. Stop thinking too much about this issue and take it as normal as urination. Avoid spending time alone. Engage in outdoor activities.
- Increase confidence level. Compare yourself with the guys who make relationships. You are good among worst.
- Give some time to get rid of this habit. Keep patience. It may take 1–2 years. But your achievement is not to put a ban on masturbation but to reach an optimum level. Reward yourself if you meet small targets.
- Develop interest in spiritualism. Make a strong feeling of God's presence everywhere. Read spiritual books and seek guidance from an expert.
- Take good amount of liquids such as milk, juice, water and protein rich diet to make-up energy loss through masturbation.
- If you still fail to control urge then seek psychiatrist assistance. It requires some drugs for small time period and you will be alright. Never lose hope and there are bigger issues in life that require more attention.

Quick Facts

- Worldwide, more than 400 million adults become infected with an STD every year.
- India has the largest number of HIV-infected people in the world: 3-5 million, 89% of whom are younger than 45.
- Every day, about 16,000 people (or nearly six million people each year) become infected with HIV

As a teen, your family may give you more responsibilities and the chance to spend more time with your friends. This extra time with your friends may put you in new or different social situations and places. With your parents not around as much, you are making more choices for yourself and will need to keep yourself safe. If you forget about your safety, your fun can quickly turn into danger. Safety rules apply to approximately all kinds of work and at every places such as home, school, market, travelling, playground, and use of mobile phones, Internet, earplugs etc. Most importantly, you need to remain cautious in making friends, dating, sharing personal information and carrying valuables

Body matures early than mind. So practice self-control if you are adolescent.

at public place. Merely following few safety rules and use of common sense can prevent you from unwanted situations.

Staying Safe With Friends

It was after school and Sakshi and her friend Aakash were hanging out at Sakshi's house. Sakshi's parents were still at work. They were bored and tried to come up with something to do. All of a sudden, Aakash came up with an idea. He said, "Let's drink. Your parents have a bottle of vodka in the freezer." Right away, Sakshi knew this was a bad idea, but she didn't want to seem boring. So, Sakshi said, "No, my parents know how much alcohol is in that bottle. If we drink any of it, I'll be grounded for life and then we won't be able to hang out. Let's watch TV instead."

Safety in School and Public Place

Every school student is a national asset. It is primary responsibility of school to ensure no child is sexually harassed in the premises. However, kids must get guidance to protect themselves from strangers. In schools, girls may become victim of sexual harassment by:

○ Sexual jokes or comments
○ Bullying
○ Touching in sexual way
○ Sending obscene picture or videos or Sexting
○ Stalking

Staying lonely can attract stranger's attention and put you in danger.

You have the right to feel safe and to be respected by your classmates and adults at school. If you ever feel afraid or threatened, tell a teacher, school counselor, parent, or other adult you can trust. Trust your instincts, pay attention to what is going on around you, and protect yourself.

Safety in Travel When You Are Alone

○ Research your destination thoroughly before your trip
○ Download safety apps on mobile phone to ensure your close relative or friend could track your location.
○ During night avoid walking alone even on busy road, hiring private vehicle or carry valuables with you.
○ Never tell anyone that you are traveling alone. Pretend that someone is with you and you are not new to this place.
○ In taxi, never take nap and prefer known routes.
○ Don't loiter during travel. Keep moving towards your destination.

Strictly adhere to safety rules when you travel alone.

- Choose your accommodation smartly. Don't believe on strangers even if they pretend to be humble or soft spoken.
- Learn self-defence techniques and educate yourself on personal safety devises. Carry *Pepper Spray* during journey.
- Don't try to look different while travelling alone. Put up sober dress and avoid jewelry.
- Don't bring attention to yourself as being a tourist.

Safety in Internet Surfing

Can I trust everything that I read on the Internet? The answer is NO! The Internet is the biggest source of information connecting every person and community in the world. With growing access to World Wide Web, almost every kind of information is shared and uploaded. Also, many users create fake profile to access secret or personal information, lure teenagers, hack websites and many such unethical practices. Therefore, users must be cautious and follow certain rules.

Avoid friendship or share information with anonymous user on net.

- Websites that end in .gov are generally reliable because they are connected with government body.
- On accessing a particular website, if automatic downloading starts, press cross (X) button and close the website. It might contain virus.
- Keep updating your computer with latest anti-virus.
- Avoid sharing your contact details or personal information on any website or online communities without verifying its authenticity.
- Many users provide fake ID and photograph on chat rooms, social media sites and even e-mails. Be alert and avoid friendship with unknown persons.
- Avoid giving your real name and other details particularly on chat rooms.
- You can receive mails from unknown sources claiming that your mobile number has been selected in a lucky draw and you need to send bank details for transfer of funds to your account. Always avoid such emails.
- In cyber café, delete all your downloads and never forget to log-off from all websites before you leave.

○ If someone says inappropriate things to you online, uploads your picture or wants to meet you in person, immediately inform your parent.

○ If you post something on the Internet, it might go viral and you may not stop it. So think before you post.

Staying Safe When Dating

Dating relationships can be a fun and exciting part of your life. It gives opportunity to share your ideas, emotions and problems and gives special chance to get to know someone. Teenagers often fantasize about indulging in dating relationship but it should happen only when you are really ready and your parents are okay with it. When you decide to start a dating relationship, it should be because you care about someone and not because other people are dating.

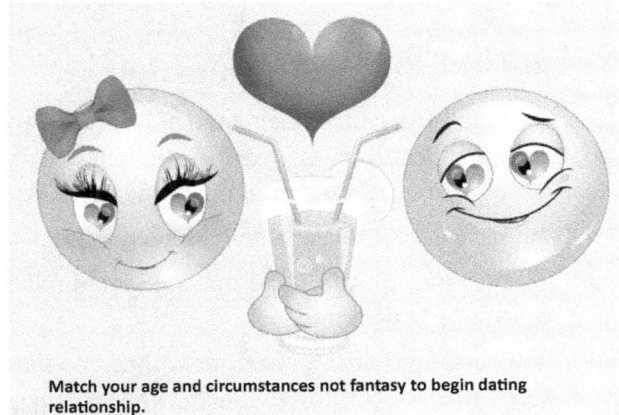

Match your age and circumstances not fantasy to begin dating relationship.

Healthy dating relationships should start with good communication, trust, and respect. As you start thinking about love and sex, do not forget to focus on feeling good about yourself. If you are serious about relationship and thinking about having sex, be mentally prepared and discuss what type of protection you would use during sex. Do not do anything that makes you uncomfortable. Respecting your right to say no means that your date will stop when you say "no." Remember that there are lots of ways to show affection other than sex.

Dating Safety Tips

○ When you go to date never forget to carry mobile phone and money with you. Always inform your parent or trusted friend about your visit.

○ Avoid sexting or sending sexy images or text to your date. It may be used to harm or blackmail you in future.

○ Deciding to have sex is a big deal, though, so think it through. Unplanned and unsafe sex can make you pregnant and create physical and emotional stress in you. So, practice abstinence when you go for dating.

○ Maybe your partner says, "If you love me, you'll have sex with me." In this situation, just think about his or her intention. Sex is not the basis of expressing love with anyone. True love involves time sharing, exchange of thoughts, feelings, and mutual respect and cares for partner's sentiments.

○ Remember that it's your body and you deserve to make your own decisions about sex. Do not feel rushed or pressured by your date in this matter.

○ Drugs and alcohol can make you more likely to do something you otherwise never would.

■ Safe Sex Practices

Sexual intercourse causes exchange of body's internal fluids between partners, it is important to realize significance of safe sex practices. If you are aware of the following facts, you can save yourself and your partner from health hazards. Here are few tips:

○ Choose low risk sexual activities such as kissing, hugging, masturbation etc.

○ The best way of safe sex is making sexual relations with one partner who has no sexually transmitted infections.

○ Avoid oral sex with the partner without condom

○ Avoid drinks and drug before any sexual activity

○ Keep genital area clean and avoid tight clothing

○ Choose minimum and trusted sex partner

○ Ensure medical check-up of both partners for STIs before sexual intercourse

Sexual violence is a broad term that includes acts of sexual assault, sexual harassment, rape, femicide (murder of women), as well as many other practices such as female genital mutilation, sexual exploitation and sexual slavery or prostitution. Sexual violence continues to be one of the most destructive social issues that crosses all social, economic, and cultural boundaries that affects men and women of every age. Despite high rate of sexual violence in society, only 6 percent cases are reported to police.

Sexual assault causes emotional effects leaving victim in stress and resentment.

Lack of evidences in sexual harassment case leads to low conviction rate. It is also one of the leading cause of suicide among women. Sexual violence takes tall on physical and mental health of victim and has destructive impacts on the lives of their families and the well-being of society as a whole. Rape and sexual assault in armed conflicts, domestic and gender-based violence, date rape, sexual exploitation of victims of natural calamities are different forms of sexual violence and human rights issues.

Quick Facts

- Research conducted by the Centers for Disease Control (CDC), USA, estimates that approximately 1 in 6 boys and 1 in 4 girls are sexually abused before the age of 18.
- 35.8% of sexual assaults occur when the victim is between the ages of 12 and 17.
- The most common first encounter of a predator with an Internet-initiated sex crimes victim takes place in an online chat room (76%).

Sexual Assault, Abuse and Harassment

There are different terminologies used to describe sexual violence depending upon nature of offence namely sexual harassment, sexual assault and sexual abuse.

Sexual harassment is bullying or coercion of a sexual nature in order to get sexual advantages. The harasser may be a woman but in most of the cases man commits sexual harassment on woman. Examples include physical contact, abusive languages, stalking, demand for sex in return for any help and sending nude images, sexting, sexual jokes or sending MMS containing explicit videos etc.

Sexual assault is an attack of a sexual nature, which includes forced sexual touching, unnatural

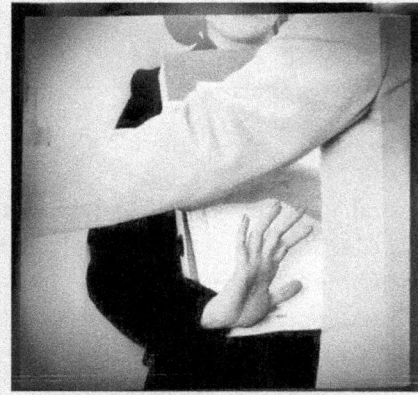

Awareness and boldness is the only arm of self-defence for women.

sex, and rape. Rape is non-consensual sexual intercourse involving forced penetration of genital or object into vagina, rectum or mouth. A rape victim may suffer physical or mental trauma and need medical assistance. It is estimated that one in three women will be raped in her lifetime. Examples of sexual assault include but not limited to rape, molestation, incest, oral and anal sex, forced masturbation, deliberately exposing private parts to someone, showing or indulging someone into pornography, unwanted kissing or touching, obscene phone calls or SMS etc.

Sexual abuse also referred to as molestation is any inappropriate and forceful physical, visual or verbal interaction for sexual stimulation or satisfaction over a prolonged period of time. It has been found that more than 90% of sexual abuse victims know their perpetrator in some way. In most of the cases, culprits were either close relative or friend. Sometimes they are so known in society that it is covered up because of the shame it can bring on their reputation.

○ Inform police, close friend or relative about the incident. Never clean your wound or place of incident, as evidence could be wiped out

○ Leave the place as soon as possible. Do not challenge or confront with the abuser directly, otherwise you could be harmed

○ Get medical treatment if you are sexually assaulted or hurt. Inform doctor about the incident for proper medical tests.

○ Refuse to be the victim. After a sexual assault, you may feel shock, embarrassment, shame, guilt, disbelief, anger, anxiety. Know you are not alone and it was not your fault.

○ Face people around you. Set example by fighting for your right and ensure culprit is behind the bars.

Common Questions About Rape

○ **If I could not resist, does that mean it is not rape?**
Many times, there are circumstances where the victim is threatened or she is mentally unstable. So, lack of consent can be considered as rape.

○ **If I used to date a person, does that mean it is not rape?**
Rape can occur when the offender and the victim have a pre-existing relationship. This is called date rape. Date can pressurize emotionally to make sexual relations and hence it can be considered as rape.

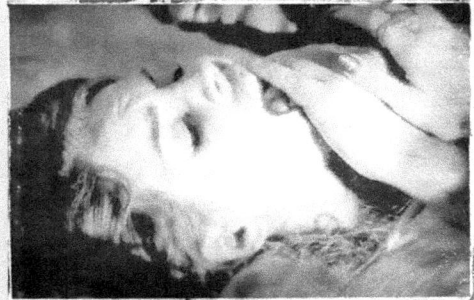

Rape tolerance impedes women's sexual rights and encourages culprits.

○ **If I do not remember the assault, does it mean it is not rape?**
Date rape drugs, which often have no smell or taste, can be given to you without you knowing at parties or in a club. Also, rape can happen when the victim was unconscious or asleep. In these cases, victim does not remember anything. So, it can be considered as rape.

○ **I was drunk, does that mean it is not rape?**
It does not matter whether you were drunk during the assault or not. If sex was non-consensual, it will be considered as rape.

Sex Abuse: Signs and Symptoms

1. Physical trauma such as redness, rashes, bruises, bleeding from oral or genital areas.
2. Trouble walking or sitting, usually as a result of pain in genital area.
3. Aggressive behavior or psychosomatic complaints such as sleepiness, excess fear, headache, mood swings etc.
4. Sudden display of interest in sexual acts inappropriate to his or her age.
5. Self-harm or suicidal tendencies, talks negative aspects of life.
6. Nightmare or other sleep problems without any explanation.
7. Sudden change in eating habits and loss of appetite.
8. Spends most of the time alone and hardly interacts with family and friends.
9. Seems distracted from normal activities including study, family function or other enjoyable activities. Skips school.
10. Develops unusual fear of particular person or place.

Tips to Prevent Sex Abuse

- Always be confident. Never show anxiety or fear to strangers
- Inform your parents where you are going, who you will be with, and when you will be back
- Learn self-defence methods to protect yourself from any attack
- Carry ID card, mobile and Pepper Spray if you are alone.
- Tell your parents about any unexpected gifts or favours you receive from friend, relative, neighbor, strangers or peer.
- Avoid visiting lonely and dark places even with your boyfriend. In crowded area also, be vigilant and remain with family and friends.

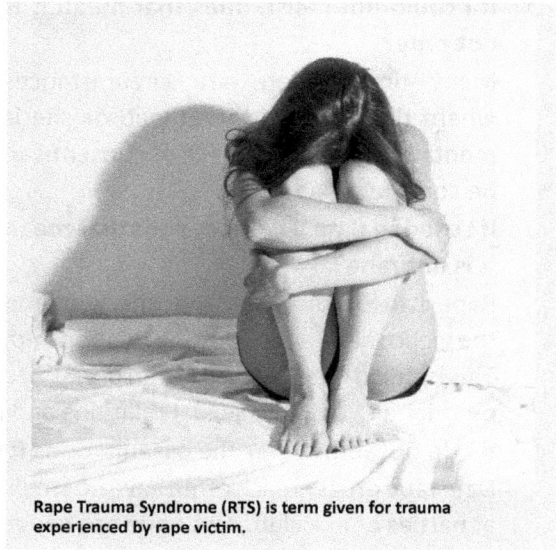
Rape Trauma Syndrome (RTS) is term given for trauma experienced by rape victim.

- Inform any elder if someone is keeping eye on you or observing your activities. Raise your voice if anybody appreciates or comments on your body parts.
- Be careful when you go out for a party or any event. Never leave your drink unattended or receive drinks from strangers. Avoid alcohol in party or pubs.
- Keep important telephone numbers such as police, hospital, friends and relatives. Memorize phone numbers of close relatives as abuser may destroy your mobile.
- Do not share your personal details such as phone number, address, email address or passwords to strangers or on social media websites. Beware of fake identity, profile and assurances on Internet.
- A young man befriends and grooms the victim into a sexual relationship by presenting himself as an 'ideal boyfriend'. After taking intimate pictures or videos, he forces the victim into having sex with friends. Hence, never allow him to record intimate moments through mobile phone.
- The offender, carefully studies your needs often offers solutions to them. They want to know your need or weaknesses and behave like they really care about you. This way, the victim sees the offender as a trusted friend. Hence, notice 'Warning sign' and be aware of their tactics.
- In order to keep the abuse secret the abuser often plays on the child's fear, embarrassment or guilt about what is happening.

Child Sexual Abuse

Child sexual abuse is a form of child abuse that includes sexual activities with a minor. Child sexual abuse does not need to include physical contact between a perpetrator and a child. It may involve masturbation, exposing private parts to child, showing porn videos, vaginal, anal or oral sex, obscene phone calls, sexting etc. The majority of perpetrators are someone the child or family knows. They can have any relationship to the child including an older sibling or playmate, family member, a teacher, a coach or instructor, a caretaker, or the parent of another child. Often the abuser uses their position of power over the victim to coerce or intimidate the

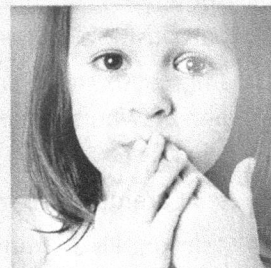

Most children are scared of reporting sexual abuse, so never avoid their silence.

child. Sometimes the child won't understand that what is happening to them is abuse. They may not even understand that it is wrong. Child sexual abuse can occur in a variety of settings, including home, school, or work. UNICEF has stated that child marriage represents perhaps the most prevalent form of sexual abuse and exploitation of girls. The effects of child sexual abuse can include depression, ADHD, post-traumatic stress disorder, sleepiness, loss of appetite, anxiety etc.

Child Grooming

Child grooming is befriending and establishing an emotional connection or luring a child with intention of sexual abuse, trafficking, indulging child into prostitution or pornography. Groomers often try to win trust of parents or victim by false promises and offering for favors. They might give gifts or money to the child for no apparent reason. Child groomers may show pornographic materials to victims as part of the grooming process. They often take advantages of family conflict, financial or health problems to win trust of family members. Sexual grooming of children also occurs on the Internet. Online grooming of youngsters is carried out via chat rooms and webcams. Sexual grooming of children over the internet is most prevalent (99% of cases) amongst the 13–17 age-group.

Do You Know?

According to US State Department, one million children are exploited in the global sex trade. Sex tourists exploit many of these children in child sex tourism. Child trafficking can occur when children are abducted from the streets, sold into sexual slavery. The greatest factor in promoting child sex trafficking and child sexual exploitation is the demand for younger girls worldwide. Children are often trafficked, employed and exploited because, compared to adults, they are more vulnerable, cheaper to hire and are less likely to demand higher wages.

Sex Abuse of Pre-School Children: What Parents Need to Teach

1. Show your kid male and female private parts using a doll or picture

2. Tell her to shout and run away from any person who tries to touch genital area

3. Ask her to always cover private parts and tell parents if she wants to go toilet

4. Ask your kid to immediately tell parents if anybody exposes or show picture or video of any sexual activity

5. Practically show different types of touch; good touch and bad touch.

Always encourage children to speak openly on sexual abuse issue.

6. Take sensible precautions with who has access to your children

7. Suggest them to find good friends and acknowledge parents if wants to go out.

8. Interact regularly with your kids and ask every detail of day-to-day activities. This will encourage child to share every good or bad experiences in life.

Sex Discrimination

Sex discrimination or Gender discrimination is treating someone unfairly on basis of person's gender. It also refers to Gender inequality differentiating men and women on basis of health, education, economic and political basis. Gender-based discrimination also involves discrimination against an individual because that person is transgender, bi-sexual, gay or lesbian. It is unlawful to harass a person because of that person's sex. Sex discrimination is the violation of human rights. Sex discrimination may occur at home or workplace. In sex-based discrimination, both victim and the harasser can be either a woman or a man, and the victim and harasser can be the same sex.

1. **Education:** Education is birthright of every citizen, however, in many countries, children are discriminated on the basis of gender. Cultural barriers, illiteracy, family responsibilities, and parent mindset prohibit girls to stand equal with boys and they are expected to play traditional roles. In the areas of less urbanization, girls are not allowed to attend school after primary level as parents do not see education of girls as 'Good' investment. Girl's quality is assessed on grounds of kitchen work, cleaning, decoration and other household works. This is the reason why female literacy rate lags behind the male literacy rate.

2. **Workplace:** Sexual harassment at workplace is a kind of sex discrimination where, harasser can be the victim's supervisor and may ask for sexual favours in lieu of incentives, promotion, transfer etc. Discrimination in different work situations include but not limited to hiring, termination, payment, job assignments, promotions, layoff, training, fringe benefits, and any other term or condition of employment. Not allowing women in certain jobs also shows occupational inequality on the basis of gender. Women also face pregnancy discrimination in jobs where, firms may not provide medical leave or salary for sickness, childbirth or recovery period. Religion-based discrimination in jobs is also illegal and punishable under law.

3. **Female foeticide:** Foeticide is the deliberate killing of foetus in the womb on the basis of gender. With advent of sex-determination techniques, female foeticide is rising despite prohibition by law. In some Asian countries, foetus or new born female are killed or dumped leading to high differences in sex ratio. Female foeticide increased drastically with arrival of ultrasound technology which provides 100 percent accuracy of sex determination. It is estimated that over 10 million female foetuses may have been illegally aborted in India since 1990. Dowry, cultural preferences, crime against women and poverty are some leading causes of female foeticide.

4. **Dowry:** Dowry refers to demand of cash, property, or gifts from bride's family from bridegroom's parents or relatives as a condition of the marriage. The dowry system in India contributes to gender inequalities by influencing the perception that girls are a burden on families. The dowry system is thought to put great financial burden on the bride's family and often leads to crime against women post marriage. Despite an unlawful act, dowry system poses a big challenge as educated families in India continue to follow this unethical practice during marriages.

5. **Violence:** Domestic violence, rape, dowry-related violence, female genital multilation, war rape, human trafficking, sexual slavery, forced prostitution, honour killing are different kinds of gender-based violence. From domestic abuse to rape as a weapon of war, violence against women is a gross violation of their human rights. The World Health Organization (WHO) has categorized violence against women in five stages: 1) pre-birth, 2) infancy, 3) girlhood, 4) adolescence and adulthood and 5) elderly. Females in first three stages are most vulnerable due to dependence on parent or guardian. Violence against women also affects physical and mental health condition putting women on high risk of any diseases. Marital or spousal rape is also a crime where non-consensual sex perpetrated by the victim's spouse. Global prevalence figures indicate that 35 percent of women worldwide have experienced either intimate partner violence or non-partner sexual violence in their lifetime.

How to Deal With Sexual Violence

Revenge Porn: The term 'Revenge Porn' is used to indicate sexually explicit contents shared over Internet or other methods by intimate partner to distort his/her image. In this way, victims may face cyberbullying or humiliation in family or work place. Revenge porn is usually practiced by ex-husband or ex-boyfriend. Revenge porn may cause severe consequences as victims' personal moments are shared with their friends or relatives causing mental stress or trauma that can lead to suicide. Images and video of sexual acts are often combined with person's private details, such as their home addresses and workplaces. Revenge porn is a kind of online sexual harassment of women. Lack of stringent laws and low conviction rate of cyber crime, is cause for increasing revenge porn cases. The perpetrators distribute victims' picture and video through emails, social media, MMS, or porn websites. This practice causes immediate, devastating, and in many cases irreversible harm to victim.

How to Deal With Revenge Porn

Prevention: It is the best option to suffer any consequences of your break-up or divorce. The culture around technology is rapidly changing and it is hard to estimate the consequences of our actions on Internet. Don't be emotional and allow recording of personal moments by your boyfriend. When you go into a relationship, you should talk to your partner about your privacy expectations and lay down some ground rules around the images you share. Once posted on website, it is very difficult to stop its spread and sharing.

Revenge Porn is a kind of digital sexual assault degrading women's image without any fault.

Legal Action: If you are a victim of revenge porn immediately contact cybercrime cell. Search and screen all your contents on the net. You can also contact websites and ask them to remove your images. You can use copyright law to take stern action against culprit.

Ask Google to Remove Content: If you find your picture or video on the net, you can send request to Google to remove such contents from websites.

8 | Schools' Role in Sexuality and Reproductive Health Education

Sexuality and Reproductive Health (SRH) Education is necessary for all age groups specially adolescents as they transition from childhood to the responsibilities of adulthood. During this period, they experience a new phenomenon associated with sexuality. Yet SRH education gets little attention in society due to cultural and political sensitivities. People often assume that young people do not need to know about SRH until they are married. This idea is rooted in traditional values and long-standing taboos surrounding

School is the best place to provide sex education with scientific and practical approach.

sexuality that need to be examined in light of protecting health. International consensus affirms that adolescents need and have a right to sexual and reproductive health (SRH) information and services. Teens often switch to TV, social media, magazines or talk with friends on SRH issues but they can perpetuate misconceptions about SRH matters. Rules about sexual behavior can differ widely across and within cultures. Therefore, providing SRH education in schools is the easiest and most practical way to reach to adolescents and discuss SRH topics. SRH education programs can be developed in all schools to provide clear, age-appropriate, and science-based sex education that is culturally relevant and grounded in the universal values of respect and human rights.

Quick Facts

- Around 22 million unsafe abortions are estimated to take place worldwide each year, almost all in low- and middle-income countries.
- According to the UNAIDS 2008 Global Report on the AIDS Epidemic, only 40% of young people aged 15-24 had accurate knowledge about HIV and transmission.
- Nearly all teens (87%) and adults (91%) agree that it would be easier for teens to delay sex and prevent teen pregnancy if teens were able to have more open, honest conversations about these topics with their parents. (source: teenagepregnancy.org)

Benefits of SRH Education in Schools

○ Messages disseminated in schools are age-specific and tailored to the students' needs.

○ Communities usually value schools and consider them to be a safe and trustworthy source of information.

○ Teachers are respected and trusted by pupils and are often role models for adolescents.

○ Students feel free to discuss sex-related issues with friends or teachers rather than parents.

The UNESCO report International Technical Guidance on Sexuality Education, produced in collaboration with four other UN agencies, stresses the need for designers of SRH programs to make cultural relevance and local adaptation a priority and to engage and build support among local opinion leaders. UNESCO emphasizes that sexuality education is not about promiscuity or encouraging young people to have sexual relationships. On the contrary, it gives young people the opportunity to explore their values and attitudes while building the skills to make decisions,

UNESCO

United Nations
Educational, Scientific and
Cultural Organization

communicate with others, and reduce the health risks related to sexuality. In response to this challenge, UNESCO in partnership with UNAIDS, UNFPA, UNICEF and WHO seeks to assist education, health and other relevant authorities to develop and implement school-based sexuality education materials and programmes.

The World Health Organization (WHO) recommends that SRH education be provided within the context of school programs and activities that promote health. School-based SRH programs are more effective when they develop life skills and have several mutually reinforcing objectives. They need to address a variety of health issues that young people may face, such as the use of tobacco and other drugs, nutrition, and the prevention of violence and of HIV/AIDS. School-based HIV and SRH education can provide the practical knowledge and skills needed to reduce adolescents' vulnerability to reproductive health problems, including HIV infection. Schools can develop capacity in adolescents to understand their sexuality in the context of biological, psychological, socio-cultural and reproductive dimensions and to acquire skills in managing responsible decisions and actions with regard to SRH behaviour.

UNICEF identifies this as a critical role for school teachers, both for helping prevent sexual abuse and for increasing the likelihood of reporting if abuse occurs. This includes giving children "clear and helpful messages about their bodies, about issues of sexuality appropriate for their age, and about dangers they may face." Providing children with a healthy attitude toward sex helps them learn to make decisions about right and wrong, build vocabulary to communicate with responsible adults, and feel less shame if they have been abused. Healthy sex education is critical for helping prevent sexual abuse and for increasing the chances of reporting if abuse occurs. With such a healthy attitude toward sex, children can learn to make decisions about what is truly right and wrong. They can develop the vocabulary to talk to responsible adults. They can feel less shame if they have been abused. To accomplish this requires education of teachers, of health care professionals and of parents.

WHO's Recommendations on Sex Education in Europe

The "Standards for Sexuality Education" were developed under the guidance of BzGA, WHO Collaborating Center and the WHO Regional Office for Europe and were officially launched in October 2010. The Standards entail framework for policy makers, educational and health authorities and specialists in specifically Eastern European and Central Asian countries. The Standards comprise a

Sex education makes your ward more responsible towards sexual relationship.

general introduction to the importance of sexuality education in school and categorised under different age groups.

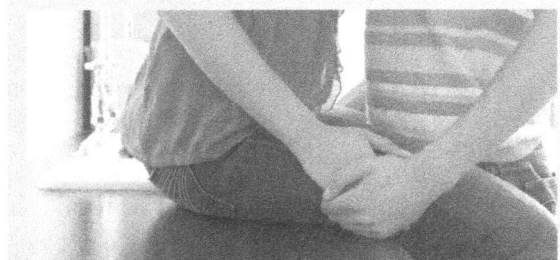

From birth to 4 years of age:

○ Informing children about the "enjoyment and pleasure when touching one's own body, early childhood masturbation".

○ Telling children about "the right to explore gender identities".

○ "Acceptance of different ways of becoming a child of a family".

○ "The awareness that relationships are diverse".

From 4 to 6 years:

○ Children should "consolidate their gender identity".

○ Being informed about "different concepts of a family".

○ Accept "diversity".

From 6 to 9 years:

○ Children should be informed about the "choices about parenthood and pregnancy, infertility, adoption, the basic idea of contraception (it is possible to plan and decide about your family)".

○ "Different methods of conception".

○ Receive information on "enjoyment and pleasure when touching one's own body (masturbation/self-stimulation)".

○ Learning about the "sexual rights of children".

From 9 to 12 years:

○ Children should have "an understanding and acceptance of changes and differences in bodies (size and shape of penis, breasts and vulva can vary significantly)".

○ "Learn about: different types of contraception and their use; myths about contraception".

○ Acquire skills on the "use condoms and contraceptives effectively in future".

○ Be informed about "first sexual experiences, gender orientation, sexual behavior of young people (variability of sexual behavior), differences between gender identity and biological sex", and "pleasure, masturbation, orgasm".

○ Have the ability to "make a conscious decision to have sexual experiences or not".

○ Accept, respect and understand "diversity in sexuality and sexual orientation".

From 12 to 15 years:

○ Receive information about "contraceptive services".

○ Learn about "pregnancy (also in same-sex couples)".

○ Acquire the skills to "make a conscious choice of contraceptive and use chosen contraceptive effectively".

○ Gender-identity and sexual orientation, including coming out/homosexuality.

○ Information on "sexual rights as defined by International Planned Parenthood Federation (IPPF) and by World Association for Sexual Health (WAS)".

15 years and above:

○ Information on "pregnancy (also in same-sex relationships) and infertility, abortion, contraception, emergency contraception (more in-depth information)".

○ Acquire "a critical view of different cultural/religious norms related to pregnancy, parenthood, etc".

○ Learn about "transactional sex (prostitution, but also sex in return for small gifts, meals/ nights out, small amounts of money), pornography, and sexual dependency".

○ A change from possible negative feelings, disgust and hatred towards homosexuality to acceptance and celebration of sexual differences.

○ Family structure and changes, forced marriage; homosexuality/bisexuality/asexuality, single parenthood.

○ Be told about the "right to abortion".

○ "Be empowered to claim sexual rights"

Source: Federal Centre for Health Education (BZgA)"

The Case of the Netherlands

In the Netherlands, sex education starts in primary school. Lessons are designed to acknowledge kids about genital organs, body awareness and pregnancy and help them understand feelings of love, compassion, hugging, good touch and bad touch. Many people believe that sex education is the source of information for sexual intercourse and contraception. However, sex education in the Netherlands enables youth to take decision on sexual matters and inspires for love and good relationship along with respect, intimacy, and safety. This is the reason why the Netherlands has one of the lowest teen pregnancy rates in the world. A study has found that approximately 90 percent of teens use protection during sex and therefore, rates of HIV infection and sexually transmitted disease in the Netherlands is quite low.

The least expensive, most useful and pleasing recreation is the study of literature on truth.

—*Sriram Sharma Acharya*

SRH Education in Muslim Countries

Tunisia was the first Muslim country to introduce information on reproduction and family planning in its school curriculum in the early 1960s. By the early 1990s, reproductive health education for both girls and boys had been incorporated into the public school science curriculum.

Impartial and age-specific sex education is global need of 21st Century.

Turkey stands out for its coverage of SRH topics in the school curriculum and the willingness and openness of teachers to discuss these issues in the classroom. Its "Puberty Project" provides sexuality education during the last three years of the eight-year primary school system, including such topics as understanding ejaculation and coping with pimples. Students receive a textbook on sexual health issues, and trained health experts visit classrooms—divided by sex and grade level—to talk to students and to answer questions. In each grade, both a male and a female teacher are trained and assigned to answer students' questions throughout the school year.

In **Iran**, all university students—male and female, regardless of their field of study—have been required since the mid-1990s to take a course titled "family planning" that covers broad reproductive health issues. More recently, a special course on HIV/ AIDS was developed as an appendix to biology books, and 13,000 teachers and school physicians were trained to educate students in high schools.

In **Malaysia** the Ministry of Education integrated SRH education into the secondary school curriculum in 1989 as a package called "Family Health Education." In December 1994, elements of this package were also introduced into primary schools curriculum as part of physical and health education. Muslim students are also exposed to sexual and reproductive health issues as a compulsory subject in Islamic education programs.

Sources: Farzaneh Roudi-Fahimi, *Facts of Life: Youth Sexuality and Reproductive Health in the Middle East and North Africa (Washington, DC: Population Reference Bureau, 2011); and Azriani Rahman et al., "Knowledge of Sexual and Reproductive Health Among Students Attending School in Kelantan, Malaysia," Southeast Asian Journal of Tropical Medicine and Public Health 42, no. 3 (2011): 718.*

PART II
INFILTRATION AND UPSURGE OF PORNOGRAPHY

9 Dirty Secrets of Pornographic World

Erotica has existed since man first was able to think. Evolving from small and secret market, pornography has now burst out as a giant in entertainment due to the Internet. Most people with access to the Internet have seen pornography either intentionally or accidentally. Pornography opens the door of fantasy world for minors whose mind is still in the process of reshaping ideas, developing imagination power, and who often tries to emulate any new act. Immature mind of youngsters accessing porn websites projects image of woman as an object or a commodity that can be used by any person. In this way, the seed of cruelty and violence is sown at

Internet is the major source of *Porn Drug* making user vulnerable to sexual addiction.

foundation stage deliberately or unintentionally. Remember, porn is a fantasy. It teaches wrong and impractical sexual acts. Porn lures immature and short-sighted viewers and evokes desires that may become nightmares for men. Pornography encourages men to have unrealistic expectations from their partners. They often try unnatural sexual activities that may hinder successful married life. Women generally hate quick sex unlike men and that is the reason why they hate porn.

Inside Story

This is an established truth of any business that need or desire increases demand, which leads to manufacturing and marketing of products. Same is the case with porn industry that has become most lucrative market of the world. Demand is created by offering free preview of erotic images, videos and cartoons in different websites. Subsequently, girls, prostitutes, porn actors are lured for new websites or movies. Most of the websites even contain movie clips recorded by hidden cameras in hotels, washrooms, and changing room. Video is recorded secretly by boyfriend and spouse and then circulated within seconds through MMS, WhatsApp, You Tube, Porn sites and other social media websites just for fun. It breaches privacy of women who are kept in dark about the circulation of video in public.

Falling in Trap of Pornography

Men often access pornographic materials in secret but most of them would deny watching erotic pictures and video in public. One of the reasons why they hide their pornographic interest is associated with the feeling of shame, which may cause embarrassment if revealed in public. Every individual wants to prove himself an ideal boy friend, a good husband and a noble citizen and considers that the truth of watching pornography might be fatal for a healthy relationship. The experience of shame is humiliating and builds negative perception about sexual issues in mind. The shameful feeling often leads to self-condemnation, causes isolation and the person considers himself as cheater. Many times, the guilt factor becomes so powerful that it costs high on studies, mental stability, health, and personal relations. Since the person wants to keep the issue secret, he avoids seeking help from any elder or expert and gradually the pornography seize control over mind by acting as cocaine of sexual addiction.

How Pornography Provokes Intense Sexual Desire

Earth has its own power of gravity that pulls all objects in downward direction. Similarly, pornographic desire, once aroused, attracts youth creating illusion of a virtual land of unlimited sex free from any personal, social and ethical boundaries. This arouses animal behavior and uncontrollable desire to satisfy sexual need any time anywhere. Unknowingly, the desperation lands the victim in the world of pornography by inciting series of immoral thoughts. Pornography alters brain chemistry by opening the door of infinite sexual desire without actually suggesting right way of sexual fulfillment. This is like driving a car on road without learning and license. The viewer gets trapped in the Internet pornography and involved in premature sexual activities. Students kill precious time in exploring porn websites, become isolated from good friends, and waste money. Gradually, they develop various physical and mental health problems such as weakness, depression, anxiety, decline of concentration and memory power, etc. Experts say teenagers often develop sexual problems like premature ejaculation, nocturnal emission, masturbation, and erectile dysfunction.

Quick Fact

In year 2002, there were around 70,000 sites dedicated to porn. In 2014, there are now 4.2 million in the United States alone.

Hidden Facts About Pornography

Open any search engine and just type XXX or porn, irrespective of your age, you can get the access of complete nudity. Irrespective of your age, you can access explicit material; all you need is a computer or smart phone with Internet connection. User gets wide spectrum of erotic stuff free of cost properly categorized and highlighted by links and contents full of slangs. Sexual and verbal abuse, bedroom secrets, hidden camera,

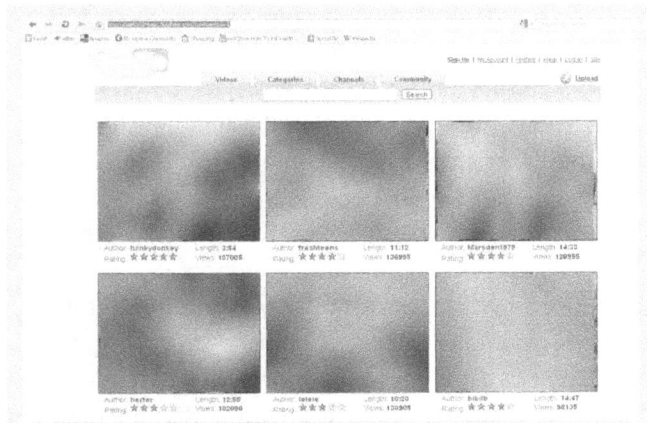

Porn websites are a click away from your kids with no censorship or restrictions.

artificially created rape scenes are few of countless sections of pornographic websites. Though pornography is a business for someone, its impact on young mind is such that it influences health, behaviour, habits, mentality and above all depicts image of women as prostitute. Do you think that anybody would like to see his wife or sister on any of these porn sites? Certainly not. Porn business is taking toll on morality of every viewer and degrading respect for women in a noble society.

Porn Websites Contents

Porn sites contain separate categories of violent, unnatural, immoral sexual acts. It provokes viewers to fantasize sex even with close relatives. The different categories include: lesbian, gay, trans-sexual, sex with animals, rape, squirt, masturbation, sex with teenagers, oral sex, anal sex, peeing, use of sex toys, group sex, sex in public, hidden cameras, sex stories, sex cartoons, sexual acts using web camera, homemade videos, sex

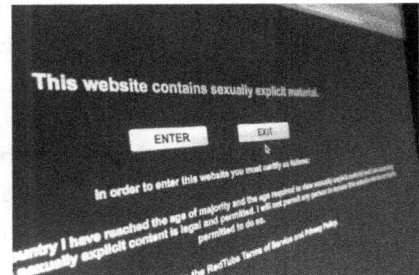

with school and college students, forced sex, sex games, sex with neighbour, amateur, old-age sex, animation, and so on. Each category contains hundreds of web pages and websites connected with each other. For instance, in hidden camera section you can find pictures and videos captured intentionally at hotels, changing room, washroom, public places including MMS recorded by a friend or spouse in good faith with spouse.

Secrets of Hidden Camera

A very small electronic camera, so small that it can be easily installed behind a light bulb, a tube light, a fixture on a wall, somewhere behind the bath room fittings or roof that's why it is called the hidden camera. This camera is mostly used to take pictures or videos of someone without his consent and knowledge mostly to victimize him for blackmailing. Sometimes hidden camera is also used by the police to carry out some nature of investigations therefore it is also called the spy camera. Now-a-days, a number of cases have

Hidden cameras are often used for secret recording of women's private moments.

been reported when criminals and antisocial elements made videos or snaps of some private moments of couples and uploaded them on the Internet.

Who Are Common Victims of Hidden/Spy Camera
1. Young girls in tailor shops trial rooms, garment shops trial rooms, changing rooms of beauty parlors, fitness centers, gyms.
2. Young couples and young single girls staying in the hotels overnight.
3. Business competitors or people having any type of rivalry.
4. People on the target of criminals or antisocial elements.
5. People on the surveillance of security agencies.

How to Detect a Hidden/Spy Camera
1. Check your smoke detector and a small led light, if it is there. Take a flashlight and shine it directly onto the grill of the smoke detector. If you see a tiny glass lens, there is a hidden camera.
2. Carefully look for any pin-sized holes in clocks, lamps and radios.
3. Carefully examine books, clocks, air purifiers, lamps and artificial flower pots or plants with the help of a flashlight. If there is any pin-sized hole, there might be a hidden camera behind it.
4. Touch any object to the mirror. If there is abnormally high separation between the object and its image in the mirror, it is double-sided. Otherwise it isn't. You can check this in household mirrors. Note that some separation is always present.
5. A hidden camera detector may be used. Many types of hidden camera detectors are available in the market, some vibrates, some give a flash light and others give a beep sound when you are in the close vicinity of the hidden camera.

Proliferation of Pornography

With the help of Internet, the access to information has become simpler and easier. But unfortunately there are also risks involved as far as our children and young ones are concerned. Minors are most vulnerable and may expose themselves to danger, knowingly or unknowingly, when using the Internet. Among these dangers, exposure to pornography is the most devastating. With rising number of porn websites, each has to compete for more viewership to sustain business and the only way to get maximum number of clicks is hardcore sex videos. This is supported by creating imagination of sex with close relatives, use of slangs, sexual violence, cheating, MMS recorded secretly and unnatural sex. Most of the

Pornography industry is one of the biggest businesses in world.

videos highlight women as slut with extreme sexual desire with the purpose of attracting more viewers. Exposure to obscene material has become common in the life of every Internet user. Whether it is any sexual advertisement found in mailbox or erotic photographs found on common websites, all such pornographic content have dominated a large part of Internet.

Internet porn industry is one of the gigantic and fastest growing businesses in the world. Earlier, pornography was restricted to magazines, books and CDs and was not readily available in the market. But the widespread public access to the World Wide Web in 1991 led to the growth of Internet pornography. Pornography is now not only available on the Internet, but also available on smart phones like the iPhone and Android, computer tablets like the iPad and Kindle Fire, and Internet television. Modern pornography is more addictive than traditional pornography due to its easy availability, explicit nature, wide range of images and videos available. The Internet is a global network and there are currently no international laws regulating pornography; each country deals with Internet pornography differently. This is the reason the porn industry is growing by leaps and bounds.

Effects of Massive Exposure to Pornography

- Men rated seven sources of sex information. The highest sources of sex information for males were (1) Friends (2) Media (3) Books and (4) Pornography. Men rated as lowest sources of information (5) School (6) Parents and (7) Church. Females rated the same seven sources of sex information.

Statistics reveal amazing truth about porn poisoning in adolescents.

  Duncan, D. & Donnelly, J. W. (1991). Pornography as a source of sex information for students. Psychological Reports, 68, 782.

- In a sample of 30 juveniles who had committed sex offenses, 29 juveniles had been exposed to X-rated magazines or videos; the average age at exposure was about 7.5 years.

  Wieckowski, E., Hartsoe, P., Mayer, A., and Shortz, J. 1998. Deviant sexual behavior in children and young adolescents: Frequency and patterns. Sexual Abuse: A Journal of Research and Treatment, 10, 4, 293-304.

- Forty percent of abused women indicated that their partner used violent pornography. Of those whose partners used pornography, 53% of the women indicated that they had been asked or forced to enact scenes that they had been shown. Forty percent of the abused women had been raped and of these, 73% stated that their partners had used pornography. Twenty-six percent of the women had been reminded of pornography during the abuse.

  Cramer, E. & McFarlane, J. (1994). Pornography and abuse of women. Public Health Nursing, 11, 4, 268-272.

- Adolescents exposed to sexually explicit websites (SEWs) were more likely to have multiple lifetime sexual partners, to have had more than one sexual partner in the last 3 months, to have used alcohol or other substances at last sexual encounter, and to have engaged in anal sex. Adolescents who visit SEWs display higher sexual permissiveness scores compared with those who have never been exposed, indicating a more permissive attitude.

  Braun-Courville, D. & Rojas, M. (2009). Exposure to sexually explicit web sites and adolescent sexual attitudes and behaviors. Journal of Adolescent Health, 45, 156-162.

- Teens who were exposed to high levels of television sexual content (90th percentile) were twice as likely to experience pregnancy in the subsequent 3 years, compared to those with lower levels of exposure (10th percentile). Teen's base rate of media consumption was measured when they were 12-17 years old and the outcome measures were taken when they were 15-20 years old.

  Chandra, A., Martino, S., Collins, R., Elliott, M., Berry, S., Kanouse, D. & Miu, A. (2008). Does watching sex on television predict teen pregnancy? Findings from a national longitudinal survey of youth. Pediatrics, 122, 1047-1054.

- Sex offenders show a high rate of use of hard core pornography: child molesters (67%), incest offenders (53%), rapists (83%) compared to non-offenders (29%). Child molesters (37%) and rapists (35%) were more likely to use pornography as an instigator to offending than were incest offenders (13%). The material used to instigate offending was often adult and consensual pornography.

  Marshall, W. L. (1988). The use of sexually explicit stimuli by rapists, child molesters and non-offenders. Journal of Sex Research, 25, 2, 267-288.

Dramatic Rise of Internet Porn Industry

- Every second US$ 3,075.64 is being spent on porn.
- Every second 28,258 Internet users are viewing porn.
- Every second 372 users are typing adult terms into search engines.
- Every 39 minutes a porn video is being created in the United States.
- 35% of all Internet downloads are porn.
- 89% of porn is created in the United States.
- 260 new porn sites go online daily.
- Daily porn search engine requests comes to a staggering 68 million, this is 25% of the total search engine request being made on the Internet worldwide every single day.
- The sex industry is estimated to gross US$ 12 billion in the United States and more than US$ 57 billion worldwide.

Source: http://www.theglobaljournals.com

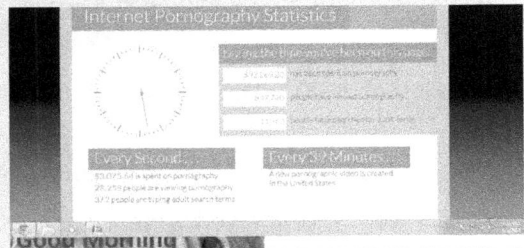

Who is Looking at Porn?

○ 80% of UK teens say porn is "too easy" to access or stumble upon on the Internet.

○ Sexting now the norm for teens.

–Times of India, June 16, 2015

○ 70% said porn was seen as normal by their peers at school.

–DailyMail, UK, August 19, 2014

○ 80% of college students in India watch porn; 40% watch rape porn.

The "digital revolution" has contributed in unexpected rise of amateur pornography.

○ 76% said that watching rape porn leads to the desire to rape a woman.

–ABP Live, India, July 24, 2014

○ Of a survey of 248 Oxford (UK) students, 71.8% of all students said they view porn

–The Oxford Student, June 12, 2014

○ 50% of Pornhub's 38 million users are viewing porn via mobile devices.

–TimesLive, June 5, 2014

○ A survey of 3000 UK families found that the average age of first exposure to pornography was 4.

○ 19% said their children got on the Internet at age 2; 38% said their kids were 3 or older.

○ 74% of parents surveyed were unaware of options to filter porn from their computers, smart phones, or tablets.

–The Scotsman, April 3, 2014

○ 56% of divorce cases had one person who was hooked on porn.

○ More than 50% of porn Internet users report losing interest in sex with their partner.

○ 40% of those who are sexually addicted lose their spouse.

○ Severe clinical depression was reported twice as frequently among porn users as compared to non-porn users.

–Christian Post, December 30, 2013

○ According to a survey of 19,000 parents, kids begin viewing porn as early as age 6.

–ABC News10, May 15, 2013

- More than 80% of Indian high school students have been exposed to porn.

  —The New Indian Express, July 30, 2013

- 90% of teenagers have viewed porn.
- 80% of 15–17 year olds have been exposed to hard core porn.
- 67% of men and 59% of women said that porn was acceptable.

  —Christian Post, July 16, 2011

- Porn users are 400% more likely to visit a prostitute.

  —The Daily Reporter, November 7, 2011

A content analysis of the 50 best-selling adult videos revealed that across all scenes:

- 94 percent of aggressive acts were committed against women.
- 3,376 verbal and/or physically aggressive acts were observed.
- On average, scenes had 11.52 acts of either verbal of physical aggression, ranging from none to 128.
- 72 percent of aggressive acts were perpetrated by men.

Incredible But True

- Porn sites cope with astronomical amounts of data. In US, 13,000 adult videos are produced annually, amassing over US$ 13 billion dollars in profit. By comparison, Hollywood released 507 movies and made only 8.8 billion.

- Every 39 minutes a new porn film is created in the United States.

- 70% of all Internet porn traffic occurs during workdays (9 am to 5 pm)

- Globally, teen is the most searched term. A Google Trends analysis indicates that searches for "Teen Porn" have more than tripled between 2005 and 2013.

Globalisation of porn industry is taking tall on women's dignity.

- In 70% of occurrences, a man is perpetrator of the aggression; 94% of the time the act is directed towards a woman.

11   Bitter Truth of Pornography

Now-a-days, female body is eroticized by media, film industry, advertisement groups, and is not only confined to Internet porn. Pornography is just a part of a huge sex industry, which includes prostitution, massage parlors, phone sex, strip clubs, escort services and sex tourism. Pornographic materials such as sexually explicit books, magazines, movies, and Internet sites amplify lust by highlighting men's domination in sexual acts. In porn sites, specific categories are designed to increase sexual cruelty,

Lack of stringent laws has led to great strides in circulation of sexually explicit contents.

and viewers try to emulate such acts either with their partners or keep the emotions intact for appropriate time. Frequent visitors of these websites become habitual of watching sexual violence on Internet. In porn movies, audience wants more extreme stuff something different from previous one. It creates a hunger to continue to purchase and objectify, and act out what is seen. In this way, pornographic materials are not just means to indulge youth in indecent activities but acting as agent of promoting sexual violence.

The increasing toxicity of pornography has wide impact on women's image as they are depicted as means of pleasure for men. Representation of women as animals, unnatural and forced sex with one or more females, women's naked body being used as tables for eating or playing cards, women subjected to different kind of sexual violence represent nasty and brutish aspect of pornography. Projection of negative image of females results in 'loss of respect' of women. For men watching porn videos, sexual act becomes a way to exercise power and dominance over women. Exposure to sexually explicit themes and scenes of cruelty in porn websites provoke mind of sexual offenders making society 'rape-prone'.

Do You Know?

- 88.2% of top rated porn scenes contain aggressive acts.
- The average life expectancy of a porn star is 36.2 years.
- Porn scenes have sexist and racist themes and websites contains categories such as interracial, teens, body types to provoke such feelings.

Porn Leads to Sexual Violence

A meta-analysis of 46 published research studies on the effects of pornography on sexual perpetration, attitudes regarding intimate relationships, and attitudes regarding the rape myth found that exposure to pornographic material puts user at increased risk for committing sexual offenses, experiencing difficulties in one's intimate relationships, and accepting rape myths (i.e. beliefs that trivialize rape or blame

Porn increases tolerance for extreme sexual acts including rape.

the victim for the crime). Specifically, there is a 22% increase in sexual perpetration; a 20% increase in negative intimate relationships; and a 31% increase in believing rape myths. A total sample size of 12,323 people comprised the present meta-analysis.

A survey of women leaving abusive male partners found that 75% were shown pornography and asked or forced to enact scenes from it; 64% had pornography described to them and were asked or force to replicate the acts; 31% had been asked to pose for pornographic pictures, and 81% had been raped. The study found a strong association between men's use of violent pornography and the physical abuse of women.

The use of pornography by 256 perpetrators of sexual offenses, all of whom were undergoing assessment and treatment, was investigated. 56% of the rapists and 42% of the child molesters implicated pornography in the commission of their offenses.

Source: https://www1.umn.edu/aurora/pdf/ResearchOnPornography.pdf

Porn and Sex Trafficking

Pornography drives the demand for sex trafficking. Sex trafficking is defined as recruiting, enticing, harboring, transporting or providing either (i) an adult for commercial sex by force, fraud or coercion, or (ii) a child for commercial sex, regardless of the means. Many women and children who are being sexually exploited and trafficked are also being used for the production of pornography. Sometimes acts of prostitution are filmed without the consent of the victim and distributed. In pornography industry, porn producers, directors, agents, pimps who recruit and entice a woman to engage in commercial sex act by means of:

- ○ **Force:** Beating, slapping, rape, beating with objects such as chain, belts, whips, etc.

- ○ **Fraud:** Lying about actual act in film, fraudulent offers of money and fame, offering false sense of security.

- ○ **Coercion:** Threats of serious harm including financial, reputational and physical assault to indulge in unnatural sex, threats of legal action to intimidate women, verbal and emotional abuse, drugs and alcohols offered to women to help them get through scenes.

▪ The Inside Story

Ex-Porn Star Jersey Jaxin writes

"You're viewed as an object and not as a human with a spirit. People do drugs because they can't deal with the way they are being treated. Seventy five percent of porn performers are using drugs to numb themselves. There are specific doctors in this industry that if you go in for a common cold they'll give you Vicodin, Viagra, anything you

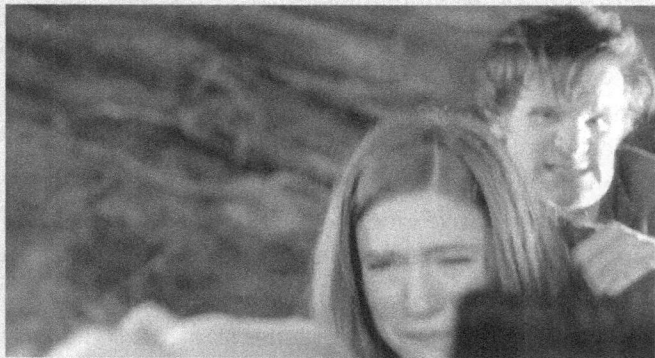

Anyone watching porn contributes to sex trafficking of women.

want because all they care about is the money. You are a number. You're bruised. You have black eyes. You're ripped. You're torn. You have your insides coming out."

Experience of Former Porn Actress Shelley Lubben

Sex-packed porn films featuring freshly dyed blondes whose evocative eyes say "I want you" are quite possibly one of the greatest deceptions of all time. Trust me, I know. I did it all the time and I did it for the lust of power and the love of money. I never liked sex. I never wanted sex and in fact I was more apt to spend time with Jack Daniels than some of the studs I was paid to "fake it" with. That's right none of us freshly dyed blondes like doing porn. In fact, we hate it. We hate being touched by strangers who care nothing about us. We hate being degraded with their foul smells and sweaty bodies. Some women hate it so much you can hear them vomiting in the bathroom between scenes. Others can be found outside smoking an endless chain of Marlboro light.

But the porn industry wants you to think we porn actresses love sex. They want you to think we enjoy being degraded by all kinds of repulsive acts. The truth, porn actresses have showed up on the set not knowing about certain requirements and were told by porn producers to do it or leave without being paid. Work or never work again. Yes, we made the choice. Some of us needed the money. But we were manipulated and coerced and even threatened. Some of us caught HIV from that coercion. Over 66% of porn stars suffer from sexually transmitted disease such as herpes, AIDS, Gonorrhea, etc. I personally caught Herpes, a non-curable sexually transmitted disease. Another porn actress went home after a long night of numbing her pain and put a pistol to her head and pulled the trigger. Now she's dead.

Former Porn Actress Shelley Lubben

It's safe to say most women who turn to porn acting as a money-making enterprise, probably didn't grow up in healthy childhoods either. Indeed, many actresses admit they've experienced sexual abuse, physical abuse, verbal abuse and neglect by parents. Some were raped by relatives and molested by neighbors. When we were little girls we wanted to play with dollies and be mommies, not have big scary men get on top of us. So we were taught at a young age that sex made us valuable. The same horrible violations we experienced then, we relive through as we perform our tricks for you in front of the camera. And we hate every minute of it. We're traumatized little girls living on anti-depressants, drugs and alcohol acting out our pain in front of you who continue to abuse us.

As we continue to traumatize ourselves by making more adult films, we use more and more drugs and alcohol. We live in constant fear of catching AIDS and sexually transmitted diseases. Every time there's an HIV scare, we race to the nearest clinic for an emergency checkup. Pornographers insist giving viewers the fantasy sex they demand all the while sacrificing the very ones who make it happen. In other words, no condoms allowed. Herpes, gonorrhea, syphilis, chlamydia, and other diseases are the normal anxieties we walk around with daily. We get tested monthly but we know testing isn't prevention. Besides worrying about catching diseases from porn sex, there are other harmful activities we engage in that are also very dangerous. Some of us have had physical tearing and damage to internal body parts.

When porn actresses call it a day and head home we attempt to have normal healthy relationships but some of our boyfriends get jealous and physically abuse us. So instead we marry our porn directors while others of us prefer lesbian relationships. It's a real memory making moment when our daughter accidentally walks out and sees mommy kissing another girl. My daughter will vouch for that one.

On our days off we walk around like zombies with a beer in one hand and a shot of whiskey in the other. We aren't up to cleaning so we live in filth most of the time or we hire a sweet foreign lady to come in and clean up our mess. Porn actresses aren't the best cooks either. Ordering food in is normal for us and most of the time we throw up after we eat because we're bulimic.

For porn actresses who have children, we are the world's worst mothers. We yell and scream and hit our kids for no reason. Most of the time we are intoxicated or high and our four-year olds are the ones picking us up off the floor. When clients come over for sex, we lock our children in their rooms and tell them to be quiet. I use to give my daughter a beeper and tell her to wait at the park until I was finished.

A closer look into the scenes of a porn star's life will show you a porn movie doesn't want you to see. The real truth is we porn actresses want to end the shame and trauma of our lives but we can't do it alone. We need you men to fight for our freedom and give us back our honor. We need you to hold us in your strong arms while we sob tears over our deep wounds and begin to heal. We want you throw out our movies and help piece together the shattered fragments of our lives. We need you to pray for us the next fifteen years so God will hear and repair our ruined lives.

12   How to Overcome Porn Addiction

Addiction is the state of being enslaved with abnormally strong craving to any act or substance that is psychologically or physically habit-forming. People are aware about addiction to narcotic drugs but youngsters with uncontrolled sexual desire often get addicted to pornography. Like cocaine, the toxic effect of porn on the teenager's brain leads to different health problems and diverts from academic growth. Depictions of group sex, sadomasochistic practices, lesbian acts, oral sex and sex with animals provoke compulsive sexual desire; and teenagers, unaware of its implications, are attracted to

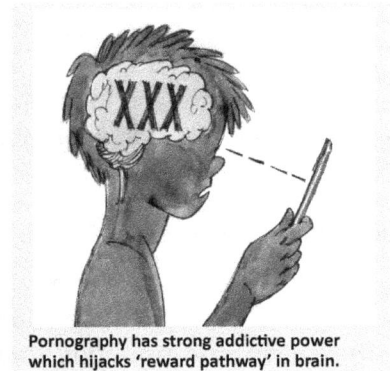

Pornography has strong addictive power which hijacks 'reward pathway' in brain.

immoral acts. Once addicted, their lust to sexual acts increases and like drug addicts, they require more and more explicit materials to feel the level of excitement felt earlier.

During certain critical periods of childhood, a child's brain is being programmed for sexual orientation. Exposure to healthy sexual norms and attitudes during this period can result in the child developing a healthy sexual orientation. In contrast, if there is exposure to pornography during this period, sexual deviance may become imprinted on the child's brain resulting in porn addiction or immoral sexual practices.

Do You Know?

- Seventy percent of 18–24-year-old youths visit pornographic sites in a typical month.
- One-fourth of all search engine requests and 35 percent of downloads are pornography related.
- There are 116,000 searches for 'Child Pornography' every day.
- The average age at which a child first sees pornography is 11.
- The entire world wide industry of porn is worth $5 billion.

(Source: OnlineSchools.org)

Dangers of Porn Addiction

Porn addiction is a disorder which gets more extreme with each passing day; it hardly gets better. At times, the addict remains under an illusion that he is in control, but the truth is he only switches from sexual release to the control of it. The control phase remains only for an hour, a week, a month, and the addict is back in the behavior again despite his promise to himself or others never to do it again. When the state of pleasure ends, the addict often regrets at his failure and switches back to the first stage of making promise for abstaining from the behavior until his resolve weakens again. The porn companies would like to see more and more get addicted to their product. For an addict, the porn is an ever-demanding product, so he asks for more and more. To get addicted, one doesn't have to shoot up any drug with a needle – body and brain will make its own drugs just by looking at the pictures.

Getting Trapped in Porn Addiction

Internet sex addiction comprises a set of five stages from use to abuse. The progression from one stage to another may be gradual or suddenly; it can happen within few days or hours after the first exposure.

The process of porn addiction is as follows:

Discovery → Escalation → Obsession → Numbness → Sexual Impulsiveness

Prolonged use of pornography disrupts child's sexual development.

(1) *Discovery* – The addiction process starts initially with the first exposure of pornography on Internet; this may be intentionally or unintentionally. For children, age 6–8, the first exposure happens unintentionally, in the form of sexual advertisements in mail boxes or on websites which are common in use. At a later age, they start actually seeking it out.

(2) *Escalation* – As person become comfortable in accessing the porn websites, he keeps coming back for more. His excitement to watch more porn escalates at this second stage. Accessing porn sites become a regular part of online activities. He gets hooked to this routine.

(3) *Obsession* – In third stage, the person's excitement to watch porn turns into obsession. He gets captivated by the porn-watching habit. He becomes obsessed and looks for more and more. He starts seeking for intense porn which could excite him more.

(4) *Numbness* – The fourth stage binds the person to numbness. Now, nothing excites him anymore; but he gets desperate badly to feel the same excitement again. This desperateness impacts his complete offline life badly.

(5) *Sexual impulsiveness* – In obsession to get the thrill back, the person adopts sexually impulsive behaviors. At this stage, many men make a dangerous jump, such as fantasizing about raping a woman. They feel the compulsivity to move from fake to real. They try to see the victim as an object who "fit" the scenario that porn had taught them to look for. With just a little more push, they try to rape and finally kill the woman.

How Porn Addiction Matches With Other Addictions

A research by Cambridge University assessed the brain activity of 19 addictive pornography users against a control group of people, who said they were not compulsive users. MRI scans of test subjects who admitted to compulsive pornography use showed that the reward centres of the brain reacted to seeing explicit material in the same way as an alcoholic's might on seeing a drinks advert. People who are addicted to pornography show similar brain

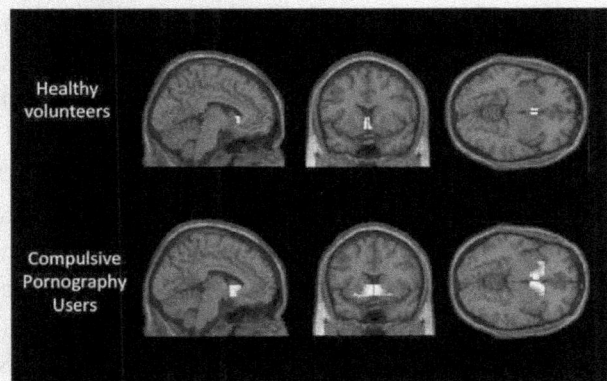

Scientists reveal changes in brain for compulsive porn users.
(*Source:* http://www.independent.co.uk)

activity to alcoholics or drug addicts, the study revealed. According to neuropsychiatrists, greater activity in an area of the brain called the *ventral striatum* is detected, which is a reward centre involved in processing reward, motivation and pleasure. When an alcoholic sees an advertisement for a drink, his brain is stimulated in a certain way. Similar kind of activity is seen in brain of porn addicts.

A man is free to do anything; but there is no choice regarding the selection of its consequences.
– *Pt Sriram Sharma Acharya*

Steps to Overcome Porn Addiction

The thing that is going to play the biggest role in overcoming porn addiction is your willingness to get rid of this menace. If you don't want to do it, then you can find so many excuses and problems. Find a reason to be more invested. Consider how it puts money, time, health problems and personal relations on stake. Once you considered porn as a source of relieving stress and now it is taking toll on physical and mental health. Porn affects working memory and as a result person becomes a poor performer at work because of brain's urge to watch porn again and again.

1. **Fix Time:** Specify minimum time period to watch porn each day. Alternatively, you can set a timer according to how much porn you think is healthy to watch. Reduce timing gradually as you attain confidence to get rid of addiction. Do not quit it suddenly. Any kind of addiction requires some time and porn is not different. Always give yourself and habit next chance if you fail to overcome porn addiction.

2. **Consider Spiritualism:** Feed your brain with positive thoughts and read spiritual books. Learn and practice meditation to enhance self-confidence. Yoga also helps in boosting physical and mental health. Spend the time saved in watching porn in these spiritual practices.

3. **Handle the Loneliness:** Loneliness can also drive people to excessive porn use. Keep yourself engaged in constructive work to divert mind from sexual desires. You can join a sports club, a reading group, music and dance class or cultivate a hobby.

4. **Change Environment:** Most of the teenagers often get trapped in bad companies either in school or neighbourhood. Avoid friends who encourage you to watch porn and clean up your computer if it's full of easily accessible files and browser ads or pop-ups that tempt you.

5. **Health Problem:** If you do have a real compulsion of porn and find it difficult to overcome, you might be suffering from psychological problem. Drugs, alcohol, and some mental disorders (like bi-polarism) also lead to hyper-sexual behavior. Take psychiatric help if have any of these problems.

6. **Avoid Your Triggers:** Boredom, loneliness, sexual thoughts, bad companion, touching private parts are some triggers that lead to frequent porn usage. Recognise and replace your triggers with more useful and effective thought process. You must enhance inner strength to reform habits and defeat forces of negative thought.

How Porn Pollutes Brain: A Scientific Perspective

Not all addictions are to drugs or alcohol. People can be seriously addicted to gambling, even to Internet porn. All addicts show a loss of control of the activity, compulsively seek it out despite negative consequences, develop tolerance so that they need higher and higher levels of stimulation for satisfaction. Addiction is a neurological disorder that affects reward system of the brain. In healthy

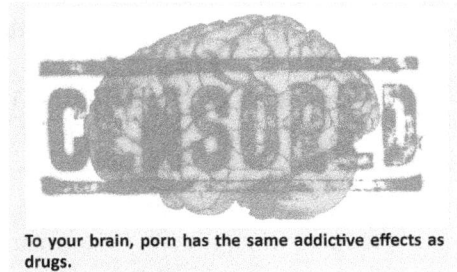
To your brain, porn has the same addictive effects as drugs.

person, the reward system reinforces important behaviour such as eating, drinking, sex and social interactions. The reward system ensures that you take your food when you are hungry and feel good, in other words, the activity of eating makes pleasurable. Sex addiction hijacks this system seizing person's natural sex need. The neural reward networks are strengthened every time the porn addict satisfies his addiction.

Nerve Connections in Brain

The human brain consists of 100 billion neurons or nerve cells, which can process 10 quadrillion (10,000,000,000,000,000) of operations (messages) per second. A typical neuron possesses a cell body (soma), dendrites, and an axon. Neurons communicate with each other through electrical impulses when the nerve cell is stimulated. Each nerve cell is attached with other with

synapses that connect an axon to another axon or a dendrite to another dendrite. Within a neuron, the impulse moves to the tip of an axon and causes the release of chemical messages or neurotransmitters that attach to receptors on the receiving cell. This process repeats from one nerve cell to another and web of communication allows you to move, think, feel and communicate.

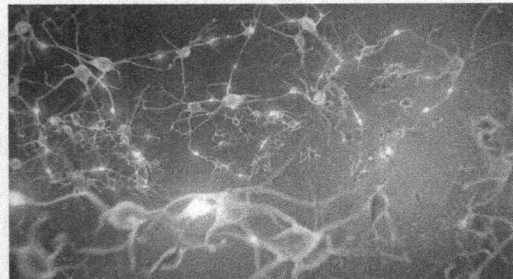
Brain contains millions of neurons carrying messages in form of signals.

Mechanism of Porn Addiction

When a neuron is stimulated, electrical impulses or action potential is generated and travels down to the axon to nerve terminal. Here, it triggers release of neurotransmitters at synapses, the gap between two nerve cells. Neurotransmitters bind through the receptors of the neighbouring nerve cell generating a signal and transferring messages from one neuron to another. There are basically three types of

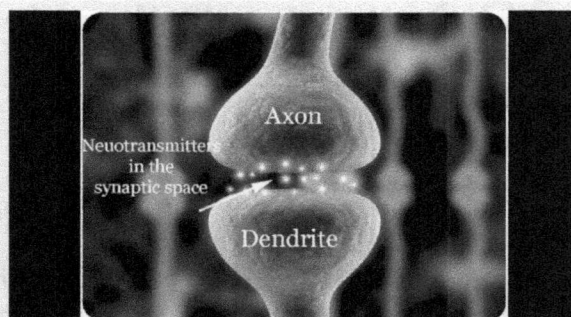

Pornography floods the brain with dopamine affecting pleasure centre of brain.

neurotransmitters – serotonin, norepinephrine and dopamine. The major reward pathways in brain involve transmission of neurotransmitter dopamine. Engagement in enjoyable activities generates action potentials in dopamine-producing neurons resulting in release of dopamine from nerve endings into the synaptic space. This means food, sex, and several drugs of abuse are also stimulants of dopamine release in the brain, particularly in areas such as the nucleus accumbens and prefrontal cortex.

Watching erotic videos or pornography regenerates more action potentials and over-stimulates release of dopamine. This can damage the dopamine reward system. Porn addicts reinforce their addiction each time they masturbate. In porn, we get "sex" without the work of courtship. Now, scans show that porn can alter the reward centre too. Once the reward centre is altered, a person will compulsively seek out the activity or place that triggered the dopamine discharge. (Like addicts who get excited passing the alley where they first tried cocaine, the patients got excited thinking about their computers). They crave despite negative consequences. Worse, over time, a damaged dopamine system makes one more "tolerant" to the activity and needing more stimulation, to get the rush and quiet the craving. As tolerance to sexual excitement develops, it no longer satisfies; only by releasing a second drive, the aggressive drive, can the addict be excited. The viewer becomes numb to things once considered pleasurable.

Some men will develop fetishes and go to specific websites or look at particular types of women. Other men will view multiple websites with different models and types of pornography, training themselves to only be aroused by lots of women doing lots of different things. Then, when they go to their one wife whose appearance doesn't change and generally keeps to the same sexual script, it doesn't arouse the man anymore. In this way, watching pornography turns into porn addiction changing laying down a powerful neurological habit disrupting viewer's thought process, family life and physical and mental health.

How Mirror Neurons Lead to Porn Addiction

What Are Mirror Neurons: Mirror neurons are nerve cells in the brain that fire during both the execution and observation of a specific action. Mirror neurons are involved in understanding the actions of others – observing an action triggers the mirror neuron system to generate a motor representation of it. They have been linked to many behaviours and abilities, from empathy to learning by imitation. The mirror neuron system transforms the visual information into knowledge of the

Mirror neurons cause imitation of activities that leads to porn addiction.

intention of the others' actions. Contagious behaviors such as yawning and itching/scratching have mirror-like properties and clearly defined stimulus and motor parameters.

The intriguing feature of many mirror neurons is that they fire not only when the animal is performing an action, such as grasping an object using a power grip, but also when the animal passively observes a similar action performed by another person. It is widely believed that mirror neurons are a genetic adaptation for action understanding; that they were designed by evolution to fulfill a specific socio-cognitive function.

Mirror neurons play major role in automatic imitation of certain activities. Automatic imitation is said to occur when observation of an action involuntarily facilitates performance of a topographically similar action (body parts make the same movements relative, not to external frames of reference, but to one another) and/or interferes with performance of a topographically dissimilar action (Brass et al. 2001; Stürmer et al. 2000). Humans show robust automatic imitation when they observe hand, arm, foot, and mouth movements (Heyes 2011). This is regarded by many researchers as evidence of a human mirror mechanism (Blakemore & Frith 2005; Ferrari et al. 2009a; Iacoboni 2009; Kilner et al. 2003; Longo et al. 2008; van Schie et al. 2008).

Sex Addiction

▸ Similar to Other Addictions
  - Dopamine surge/High
  - Cravings
  - Triggers/Conditioned Stimuli
  - Brain changes (Worse with younger age)
  - May start as recreational
  - Relationship, Financial, Emotional Problems

Mirror Neurons and Pornography

Why do humans (especially men) get so excited by seeing someone else have sex? At first glance, the answer seems obvious: watching porn triggers an idea (we start thinking about sex), which then triggers a change in our behavior (we become sexually aroused). This is how most of us think about thinking: sensations cause thoughts which cause physical responses. Porn is a quintessential example of how such a thought process might work.

But this straightforward answer is probably wrong. Porn does not cause us to think about sex. Rather, porn causes to think we are having sex. From the perspective of the brain, the act of arousal is not preceded by a separate idea, which we absorb via the television or computer screen. The act itself is the idea. In other words, porn works by convincing us that we are not watching porn. We think we are inside the screen, doing the deed. Mirror neurons facilitate this process by allowing the brain to automatically imitate the actions of somebody else. So if I see you smile, or lick an ice cream cone, or do something X-rated, then my mirror neurons light up as if I were smiling, or licking an ice cream cone, or doing something X-rated. We mirror each-others' movements, which allow us to make sense of all these flailing limbs and contorted muscles.

In the paper, published in *Neuroimage*, a Journal of Brain Function, the researchers flashed images of aroused genitalia to both men and women, heterosexuals and homosexuals. As expected, brain activity correlated with sexual preference: the minds of homosexual men mirrored the minds of heterosexual women, and vice-versa. But what really interesting was the pattern of activation itself. When subjects looked at porn in the fMRI machine, it was found that the *ventral premotor* cortex, which is a key structure for imitative (mirror neurons) and tool-related (canonical neurons) actions, showed a bilateral sexual preference-specific activation. This suggests that viewing sexually aroused genitals of the preferred sex triggers action representations of sexual behavior.

When Emotions Hijack Thinking

It is widely observed that adolescents easily develop the habit of porn watching, which is linked with emotions. The brain controls emotions through the limbic system consisting of amygdale, which plays a large role in emotional memory formation and storage. Adolescents have less control over their emotions and tend to take less matured decisions as compared to adults because the neurons of the prefrontal cortex that provide much of our rational control over emotions do not mature until early adulthood. In contrast, the amygdala is mature at birth and thus exerts a heavy influence on their emotional response. Therefore, efforts should be made to curb wide circulation of pornographic materials among teenagers.

Pornography and Neuroplasticity

Neuroplasticity is the internal ability of the brain to change, for better or for worse, throughout the individual's life span. It involves forming neuronal connections in response to information derived from new experiences in the environment, sensory stimulation and normal development. Contrary to common understanding, the brain does change throughout life. Brain volume quadruples between birth and adulthood; most of this increase in volume

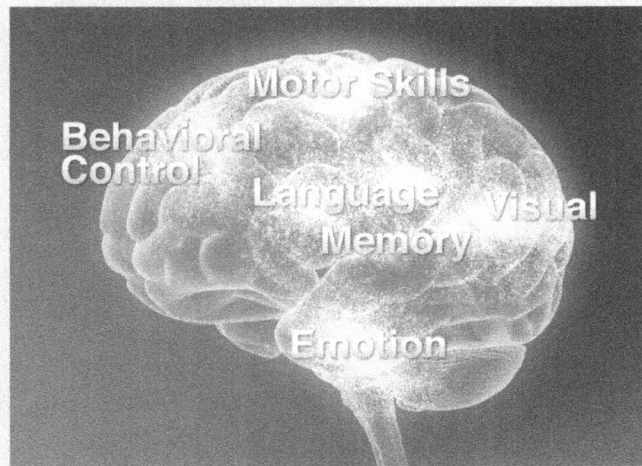

Porn lays down strong neuro-pathways making withdrawal more difficult.

comes from increased numbers of synapses (synaptogenesis), myelination of axons, and increased dendritic branching. Overproduction of synapses in the young brain may contribute to its greater plasticity. It has only been recently appreciated that the adult brain is capable of considerable plasticity.

Neurodevelopment results from an interaction between neurons and their environment. If the child is exposed to positive environment, neuroplasticity leads to development of new skills, better cognition, improved motor control and improved memory. However, if the child is kept in negative environment such as pornography, stress, crime, drug abuse etc., neuroplasticity causes impaired performance of daily activities, altered motor control, decline in brain function and amplified perception of pain. Therefore, an individual who is exposed to porn and the process is repeated, new neural circuits are formed in the brain causing addiction to pornography due to long-term and sometimes lifelong neuroplastic change in the brain.

Quick Fact

- Each single brain neuron has from 1,000 to 10,000 connections with other nerve cells.
- Brain processes approximately 70,000 thoughts per day. A new brain connection is made between two or more brain cells each time you have a new thought or memory.

How Porn Addiction Leads to Genetic Changes

Neuroscientists have revealed that all addictions, both chemical and behavioral, appear to share a key molecular switch DeltaFosB, a protein found in specific brain regions, which triggers a series of transcription events that ultimately produce an addictive state. Chronic overconsumption and associated dopamine spikes cause DeltaFosB to accumulate gradually in key areas of brain. In the *nucleus accumbens*, it functions as "master control protein" in the development of an addiction.

Studies in inducible transgenic mice support the view that DeltaFosB functions as a type of sustained "molecular switch" that gradually converts acute drug responses into relatively stable adaptations that contribute to the long-term neural and behavioral plasticity that underlies addiction. DeltaFosB has been identified as playing a central, crucial role in the development of many forms of behavioral plasticity and neuroplasticity involved in both behavioral addictions (associated with natural rewards such as pornography) and drug addictions. In the brain's reward system, it is linked to changes in a number of other gene products, such as CREB and sirtuins.

Excess chronic consumption
(dopamine surges)

⬇

Binge mechanism
(Delta-FosB accumulates)

⬇

Cravings for more

⬇

Continued consumption

⬇

Structural brain changes

DeltaFosB may accumulate within neurons of the nucleus accumbens and dorsal striatum (brain regions important for addiction) after repeated administration of many kinds of drugs of abuse in response to compulsive behaviors such as pornography, gambling and exercise. Importantly, DeltaFosB persists in neurons for relatively long periods of time because of its extraordinary stability. Therefore, DeltaFosB represents a molecular mechanism that could initiate and then sustain changes in gene expression that persist long after drug exposure ceases.

DeltaFosB increases the rewarding qualities a specific stimulus. If you are having sex with a real person, and DeltaFosB increase, cues associated with a real person will be more exciting. On the other hand, if you masturbate, the screen becomes more exciting. This all depends on perception of course. We can see why rewiring is so important — because DeltaFosB is the molecule of rewiring rewards. DeltaFosB causes sensitization — the core addiction related brain change.

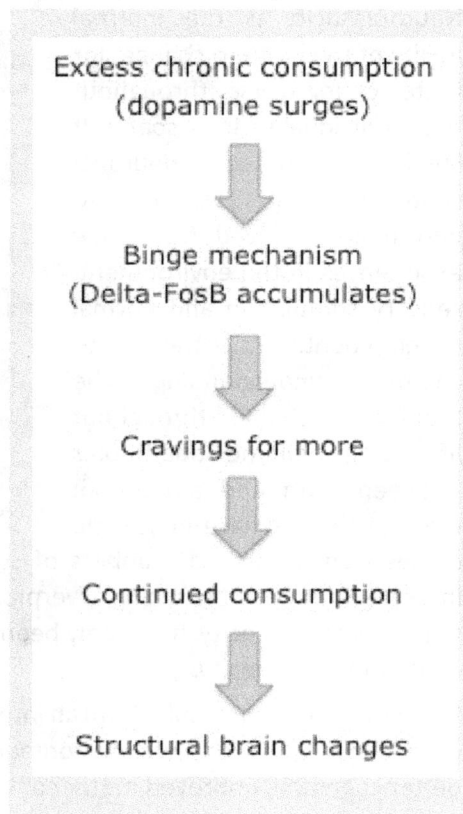

Steps to Remodel Brain

(1) Develop Positive Thoughts: Your thoughts form your character, how you operate in the world, how far you travel mentally, physically, and spiritually. You are what you think you are, and all of your actions proceed from thoughts. Happy thoughts and positive thinking support brain growth, as well as the generation and reinforcement of new synapses, especially in your prefrontal cortex (PFC), which serves as the integration center of all of

Lifestyle changes and strong will-power can free you from porn addiction.

your brain–mind functions. Negative thinking slows down brain coordination, making it difficult to process thoughts and find solutions. Thus, the more you focus on negativity, the more synapses and neurons your brain will create that support your negative thought process. Excitation, depression and abrupt agility of mental domain need to be consistently controlled and avoided. The frequent disturbances due to haphazard thinking and emotional variation are the major causes of such negative effects and fuming of the major causes of such negative effects fuming of the mental energy.

Positive Thoughts:

○ Stimulates the growth of nerve connections.

○ Improves cognition by increasing mental productivity.

○ Improves your ability to analyze and think.

○ Affects your view of surroundings.

○ Increases attentiveness.

(2) Adopt Good Practices: Brain is like a machine, it processes data like a computer and gives output based on input. More practice or repetition is done, more strong the neural circuits is formed in the brain. Much like a muscle, the more you exercise the prefrontal cortex, the stronger it becomes. Meditation is a good example of noble practice aimed to make the brain sharp, peaceful and energetic. This new habit will increase your dopamine and dopamine receptors. Making a habit of meditation has been shown to increase dopamine release up to 65%. Even after only 11 hours of meditation spread over a month, changes are observable. Meditation has been linked to cortical thickness and the density of gray matter. Long-term and short-term practice of meditation resulted in different levels of activity in brain regions associated with qualities such as attention, anxiety, depression, fear and anger. Mediation also demonstrated an effect on the ability of the body to heal itself.

(3) Positive Environment: A person develops thought, mentality, habits and culture according to environment in which he spends most of the time. Friends, relatives and neighbours play crucial role in personal development. A positive environment motivates you the best, fills you with the enthusiasm and excitement whereas the atmosphere surrounded by immoral, illiterate and criminals make us vulnerable to develop bad habits. Porn-watching is an anti-social habit. By reforging connections to real people, spending pleasurable time together, you will establish new neural pathways of pleasure. This will create compulsive behaviour and unnatural urge for sex. Suppression of erotic thoughts could lead to mental illness such as anxiety or depression whereas expression could make you anti-social or indulge in cyber crime. Therefore, if you really want to change yourself, you must try to make your group, community and society free from pornography.

Pornography Causes 'Hypofrontality'

Neuroscience now knows that willpower is a function of the prefrontal lobes of the brain. When our prefrontal lobes are working properly, then we have "executive control" of the processes going on in our brains. It is where we do our abstract thinking, make goals, solve problems, regulate behavior, and where we suppress emotions, impulses, and urges. Scientific studies have also confirmed that using porn over and over actually reshapes these areas of the brain, literally eroding our willpower and our moral compass. Neuroscientists call it hypofrontality. Hypofrontality is a state in which there is decreased blood flow to the prefrontal lobes of the brain. Hypofrontality is observed in schizophrenia patients, and is also observed in all manner of addictions. The porn-addicted brain has trouble thinking logically. When impulses and desires come from the midbrain, instead of being moderated, the brain feels these desires as compelling needs. The prefrontal region is supposed to be able to weigh consequences and situations and judiciously shut down cravings, but hypofrontality means the addict's ability to do this is impaired. This is the reason why many porn users feel focused on getting to porn and masturbating even when a big part of them is saying, 'Don't do this.' Even when negative consequences seem imminent, impulse control is too weak to battle the cravings.

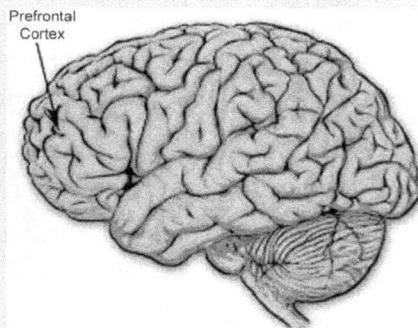

14   Teens and Sexting Behaviour

Proliferation of smartphone *culture* has provided platform for transfer of text, images and videos with affordable and anonymous methods. Most popular use of smartphone is entertainment, which is now-a-days unfortunately misused by immature minds in the form of sexting. Sexting is the act of sending or receiving a sexually explicit text, photo or video using mobile phone or instant messenger. A growing number of studies on adolescent mobile communication report that the distribution of regular pornographic images through mobile phones is a fairly common practice among teenagers. The greatest amount of concern has focused on "sexting" or the creating, sharing and forwarding of sexually suggestive nude images by minor teens. Most of the teenagers share sexually explicit messages in fun or faith but recent survey has highlighted wide implications on studies, personal relationship and morality. Sexting is often used to take revenge by defaming a particular person or group.

> I'll just let you use ur imagination for that one:)
>
> You knoww..I'm not feeling very creative right noww
>
> Let's just say we'd be up all night;)
>
> All night? Damn what could we be doing for that long..
>
> Watching movies and playing board games....

Do You Know?

- 80% of teens involved in sexting are under the age of 18.
- 39% of teens admit sharing intimate images.
- 61% of all sexters who have sent nude images admit that they were pressured to do it.

Think Before Pressing "SEND"

It will no longer be private – Once anything, text or photo, is sent or posted, it could become viral in few hours. After that it will no longer be in control. Experts say that these pictures could be collected by pornographers and finally would end up on porn sites. According to a survey, 40% of teens and young adults say they have had a sexually suggestive message (originally meant to be private) shown to them and 20% say they have shared such a message in friend circle.

Teens often take sexting causally as they are unaware of consequences.

It will be always there – Anything that is posted or sent will truly be always online. Something that is done as a joke will have its negative consequences for whole life. Your parents, teachers, relatives, friends, enemies and others may all be able to find your past posts, even after you choose to delete them. You cannot control other people's comments posted on it. Even if you have second thoughts and delete a racy photo, there is no telling who has already copied that photo and posted it elsewhere.

Do not do something under pressure – Don't come under pressure of anyone, whether it is your best friend or the person you are in love with, to do something that makes you uncomfortable, even in cyberspace. Many times in an act of revenge, if a relationship breaks up or a friend becomes angry, the pictures are often mass distributed.

It could lead to cyberbullying – Viral nasty messages or photos could also become one of the reasons of cyberbullying. There are many real-life stories of young girls who have faced cyber bullying after their objectionable photos got public. If these images come into a wrong hand, it could become a tool for blackmailing. So, anything which started as a joke today shouldn't become a reason for repent tomorrow.

Consider your dignity – Before posting or sending any racy photo, just think about your dignity in front of the one receiving or seeing it. It is easier to be more provocative or outgoing online, but whatever you write, post or send does contribute to the real-life impression you are making.

What Should Parents Do?

Lack of parents' awareness about the threats of modern technology keeps them in dark about the shocking experiences of their children. In most of the cases, children are hesitant to tell their sufferings to parents either under threat from the bully or out of fear of social disgrace. This leads to emotional, psychological and physical stress on child. In extreme cases, victims suffer mental problems such as depression, anxiety and often compelled to commit suicide. As parents, we should know what's going on, and how to protect them.

Parents need greater involvement with their wards to prevent from cyber threat.

(a) **Keep a check:** As a parent, it is your right and duty to keep a check on mobile phone of your ward. Teens often take vulgar jokes and images casually but it is how they are diverting themselves to pornography. As parents, you should trust your child but it is good to always verify their online activities. Till your children are minors, make sure that you have their current passwords and review periodically their email accounts and their Facebook page. Do not give in to the social pressure that you should let your 13-year-old "have their space."

(b) **Talk openly about it with your teens:** Too often we hear parents say, "Not my kid," or "My kid would never do that." Avoid this myth and keep your lines of communication open with your children. Once your child enters into a teen age, it is a high time that you should talk to them as a friend about the dangers of sexual involvement, dating and relationship issues.

(c) **Teach them about modesty:** Help your child see their bodies not as something to be exploited or used, but as something to be respected. Teens with a healthy attitude toward personal modesty will be much less likely to see sexting as an acceptable option.

(d) **Establish consequences:** Fathers, especially, should be stricter when behavioural rules are broken and expectations violated. On such situations, taking strict measures like cutting on Internet access, taking cell phones and banning contact with friends would ensure the safety of your child. Make sure that these consequences are understood by your teen up front.

(e) **Use Apps to monitor online and phone activities:** There are several programs out there that will allow you to monitor the use of the cell phones in your household, even to the point of getting a report of all text messages sent and received.

(i) mamaBear – MamaBear has a feature to keep watch over your child's Facebook feed. You will be alerted to any signs of bullying or use of crude language as well as when they check-in or get tagged on their friends' photos.

(ii) MobileKids – This will help you to receive alerts when your kids have been using their mobile phones in the middle of the night, when they add a new unrecognized contact, or when they download a new app. You will also get statistics about their children's mobile usage, which they can use to set usage limits.

(iii) Teensafe – This app can monitor user's phone without their ever knowing about it, and gives you an all access pass into all text messages (including deleted ones), their web history, their call logs and Facebook and Instagram feeds. You can also use GPS to track their every move.

Role of School

Schools may consider following steps to check sexting and cyber bullying:

○ School authorities are generally ignorant about cyber bullying, sexting and other cyber crime. With astonishing spike in sexual harassment cases, it is suggested to form cyber crime cell in school to check any such incidents. The victim of cyber bullying or sexting should be encouraged to report such incidents.

○ Kids who are harassed after a sexting incident need to be monitored for extreme behavior changes so that the incident may not affect their mental health and studies.

○ Schools should aware students about dangers and consequences of sexting. Sex education is an effective way to address sex-related issues.

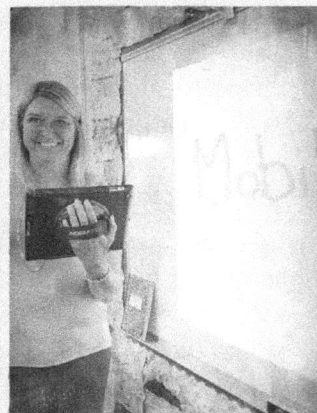

Educating teens on cybercrime is the only method to secure their life.

○ Since most sexting incidents occur at schools, parents must collaborate with school authorities to help curb sexting and ensure positive atmosphere in campus where their ward get education.

○ Teachers should be trained to provide counseling to victims of sexting or cyber bullying incidents.

○ Installation of CCTV camera in school campus is most effective way to curb any immoral conduct including sexting.

Tackling Threat of Cyberbullying

Cyberbullying is a form of repetitive aggression intended to defame, humiliate or threaten an individual or group using information and communication technologies (ICT), such as e-mail, messengers, mobile phones (SMS, MMS, phone calls), chat and social networking websites. Most common cyberbullying cases include morphing and circulating photos or videos of the victim on social networking websites, blackmailing the victim, rumouring false news through fake public profiles about any person or act of maligning someone by posting defamatory messages. Cyberbullying is especially prevalent in middle school kids (9–14). The recent use of mobile applications and rise of smartphones have yielded to a more accessible form of cyberbullying. The practice of cyberbullying is not limited to children. When perpetrated by adults, the practise of harassing others is called cyberstalking. A cyberstalker relies upon the anonymity afforded by the Internet to allow them to stalk their victim without being detected. Cyberstalkers use email, sexting, Facebook, Twitter, and other social media websites to track someone's personal information.

Girls are about twice as likely as boys to be victims of cyberbullying.

Do You Know?

- Over 80% of teens use a cell phone regularly, making it the most common medium for cyberbullying.
- One out of four becomes victim of cyberbullying.
- Researchers have found that 28% victims of cyberbullying considered suicide as compared to 22% who were physically bullied.

Different Methods of Cyberbullying

Harassment

- Sending text messages on phone and instant messengers, and emails repetitively to harass, insult or threaten the victim.

- Posting false rumours, threats or defamatory information on social networking sites.

- Joining text attacks with bullies to send thousands of text messages to the target.

Sharing personal information on social media can be dangerous.

Masquerading

- Creating a fake profile with a similar screen name of victim and then posting objectionable pictures and texts to defame the victim.

- Breaking the password of victim's profile at different social networking websites and offending the victim's friends or acquaintances.

- Setting up a fake profile with misleading information like age, sex, etc., to trap the young girls, particularly, for blackmailing.

- Posing as the victim and sharing the personal information in various chat rooms of known female molesters or hate groups, with a motive to humiliate the victim.

Defaming

- Spreading nude or degrading photos of the victim via mass emails or text messages; this is known as sexting. In this way, the photos get distributed to masses in just a few hours.

- Clicking nude or objectionable pictures of the victim and blackmailing the victim by threatening to share those photos.

- Posting those pictures on various websites with a motive to defame the victim.

Creating Websites, Blogs, Polls

○ Making a defamatory blog with a motive to insult, embarrass, or humiliate the victim.

○ Creating a website about the victim which contains the nude photos or false information.

○ Revealing the secret or confidential information with an objective to make it public.

○ Conducting an Internet poll about the victim to embarrass or humiliate her.

○ Sending viruses, spyware or hacking programs to the victim in order to spy on the victim or control his or her computer remotely.

Steps to Prevent Cyberbullying

Educate the children about responsible online behaviour – Children should be educated about the negative consequences of posting personal information and photos online, and a proper training should be given on how to take extra care in their Internet activities. A further step could be to integrate the specific lessons on cyberbullying in school curriculum, workshops, open discussions, presentations, etc. could also be arranged.

Change the school climate – To stop cyberbullying, schools should work to change the social norms and values of the school. Educating children and teens about the responsible online behaviour and the legal ramifications of it should be included in school's policy. A 'zero tolerance' policy should be adopted. It's important for students and staff to understand how cyberbullying is different from physical bullying and how it can affect others. They should be made aware that cyberbullying can be more painful than physical bullying.

Involve the kids in combating cyberbullying – Involving the kids to combat cyberbullying is another important step. Focus groups of students under the supervision of teachers should be set up, where students can come up with recommendations for what school, teachers and other students can do to change the climate of the school so it no longer tolerates bullying.

Immediate Steps

- Do not respond to cyberbullying messages.
- Keep evidence of cyberbullying. Record the dates, times, and descriptions of instances when cyberbullying has occurred.
- Sign off and block the person who is cyberbullying.

Harmful Effects of Cyberbullying

Cyberbullying leads to mental problems like anxiety, fear, depression and low self-esteem in kids. In extreme cases, these could lead to suicidal attempts also. Here are few emotional, psychological and physical effects on cyber bullied child.

Fear – Victims no longer feel safe anywhere. A feeling of invasion by bully at any place whether home or school leads to fear. Sometimes, bully hides his identity which escalates the situation more.

Victims are at greater risk for anxiety, depression, and other stress-related disorders.

Insult – As the victim knows that bullying has spread and circulated to masses, so a feeling of insult and humiliation arises. The child starts avoiding everyone.

Anxiety and depression – Victims of cyberbullying often succumb to anxiety, depression and other stress-related conditions. They often fall ill and experience headache, stomach-ache or other physical ailments. They begin to lose interest in their social life and start avoiding interaction with family and friends. Additionally, their eating habits and sleep patterns change frequently making the condition more critical.

Loneliness and isolation – Cyberbullying often leads to a feeling of loneliness and isolation among teens. This becomes more painful when they don't have friends at school.

Disinterest in academics – Cyberbullying victims often skips going to school because of the embarrassment and humiliation caused by the messages or posts shared. As they find it difficult to concentrate or study because of the anxiety and stress, their grades suffer.

Suicidal – Thoughts of suicide dominates among cyber bullied teens, as this seems to be the only way to get rid of the repetitive psychological and emotional pressure.

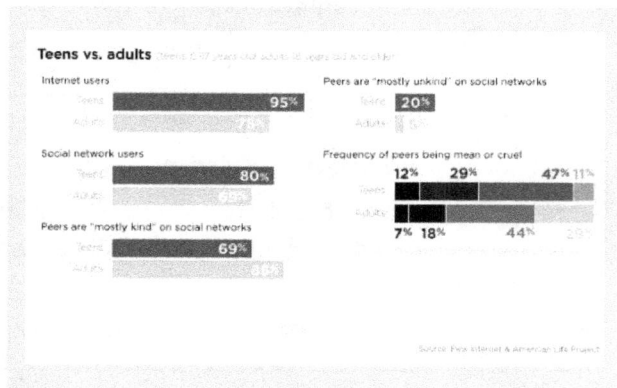

How to Know if Your Child is Victimized

As a parent you should know that your kids may not want to tell you that they are being bullied. Studies show that only 5% of children tell their parents and teachers if they are a victim of cyberbullying. Their self-esteem and self-confidence all take huge hits when bullying is involved. Youth who were bullied had found to have three times more suicidal thoughts or inclinations. Also, youth who are bullied may retaliate more often through violent actions. Parents must be vigilant about change in child's behaviour and address the issue if child or student shows any of the below signs or symptoms:

Cyberbullying can take place on social media sites such as Facebook, Myspace, and Twitter.

Changes in behaviour

- ○ Feels lonely and sad
- ○ Becomes secretive about Internet activities
- ○ Changes in sleeping patterns
- ○ Losses interest in social events
- ○ Misbehaves frequently
- ○ Seems upset after reading text message on phone or accessing Internet
- ○ Have lower self-esteem

Changes in academic life

- ○ Ignores discussing school life
- ○ Skips school frequently
- ○ Receives poor grades

With rapid change in society, the mindset of teenagers is also changing. They are at the age to explore new horizons of life and curious to understand the changing world. When it comes to pornography, most parents either avoid difficult questions or shy away from hard facts. In this scenario, the teens seek more satisfactory answers from their peers or friends. It is the primary responsibility of parents to provide factual answers with scientific evidences to teens on topics related to sex education and pornography so that they are not misguided by anybody. They need to know 'why' pornography is harmful and how it can negatively impact the rest of their academic and social lives.

How to Counsel the Victim?

Once you get to know that your child has become the victim of cyberbullying, your patience and way to handle the situation become very critical. As the victim happens to be in a susceptible state, so your response towards your child and action to encounter such an unfortunate situation play an important role in either making the problem stop, or worsening the situation.

i. **Listen to your child patiently** – Your very first task is to make your child comfortable in telling everything honestly and openly to you. Listen to your child without any prior judgment, blame, or attempting to jump in and 'solve' it. Softly, try to find out when it started, since how long it's been going on, the names of those involved, and the way it has been done. If evidence of the cyberbullying is available – saved text messages, posts, websites, etc. – have your child show these to you and save these for documentation should it be needed.

ii. **Ask your child not to retaliate** – Let the child tell you honestly about any forms of retaliation he may have taken. Let him know that he will be in a worse situation if the truth happens to be different from what is told. If there is evidence of their actions, document these as well.

iii. **Recognize your child's pain** – Tell the child that you can understand or feel the pain he is going through and what happened wasn't fair. As the child is already going through a psychological trauma, so avoid saying or doing anything that makes your child feel any more isolated.

iv. **Consult the legal expert** – Depending on the severity of the situation, report the incident to police or consult the legal expert.

v. **Help your child to combat psychological distress** – Help your child to overcome the trauma of loneliness, fear, low self-esteem by counselling. Ensure that the child's studies or behaviour is not affected by distress. Parents and schools must work together to create positive environment.

16 Beyond Tolerance: Internet Child Pornography

Child pornography is exploitation or sexual abuse perpetrated against a child including infants for the production of pornography. Internet is being highly used by its abusers to reach and abuse children sexually, worldwide. In physical world, parents know the face of dangers and they know how to avoid and face the problems by following simple rules and accordingly they advice their children to keep away from dangerous

Child abuse makes children vulnerable to commit similar offences in future.

things and ways. But in case of cyber world, most of the parents do not themselves know about the basics in Internet and dangers posed by various services offered over the Internet. Hence, the children are left unprotected in the cyber world. Pedophiles take advantage of this situation and lure the children, who are not advised by their parents or by their teachers about what is wrong and what is right for them while browsing the Internet. Those distributing child pornography are employing more sophisticated security measures to elude detection and are being driven to hidden levels of the Internet. A wide movement is working to globalize the criminalization of child pornography issue, including major international organizations such as the United Nations and the European Commission.

Pornography Leads to Paedophilia

Paedophilia or pedophilic disorder is a psychiatric disorder in which an adult or older adolescent experiences a primary or exclusive sexual attraction to prepubescent children aged 13 or younger. It is estimated that 25% to 50% child molesters suffer from pedophilia. Pedophiles lure the children by distributing pornographic material and then they try to meet them for sex or to take their nude photographs including their engagement in sexual positions. Pedophilic viewers of child pornography are often obsessive about collecting, organizing, categorizing, and labeling their child pornography collection according to age, gender, sex act and fantasy.

How Pedophiles Trap Children

According to the US Department of Justice, over one million children have been sexually abused for pornography. They also note that a single offender arrested in the UK possessed 450,000 child pornography images, and that a single child pornography site received a million hits in a month. In a study analyzing men arrested for child pornography possession in the United States over a one-year period from 2000 to 2001, most had pornographic images

Sex offenders accept that viewing hard-core pornography led to child sexual abuse.

of prepubescent children (83%) and images graphically depicting sexual penetration (80%). Approximately 1 in 5 (21%) had images depicting violence such as bondage, rape, or torture and most of those involved images of children who were gagged, bound, blindfolded, or otherwise enduring sadistic sex. According to a paper from Mayo Clinic, a medical research group based on case reports of those under treatment, 30% to 80% of individuals who viewed child pornography and 76% of individuals who were arrested for Internet child pornography had molested a child.

Do You Know?

- In a survey of over 4000 readers of the women's magazine Cosmopolitan in the UK, 13% of respondents reported having been sexually abused as children by different family members and by their friends in a range of different circumstances many of which involved pornography. In Germany, police have estimated that 130,000 children are forced by parents or other close acquaintances to participate in the production of pornography.
- According to a US Children's Homes report, the number of Internet child pornography images has increased 1500% since 1988. Approximately 20% of all Internet pornography involves children, and more than 20,000 images of child pornography are posted on the Internet every week.
- It is estimated that child pornography has become a $3 billion annual industry.
- In 1996, U.S. Postal Service announced that Mexico City was one of the leading producers of child pornography videos (Inter Press Service, 10 February 1998).

Kinds of Child Sexual Abuse

○ **Nudist:** Pictures of naked or semi-naked children.

○ **Erotic Posing:** Deliberately posed pictures of fully, partially clothed or naked children in provocative poses.

○ **Explicit Sexual Activity:** Pictures that depict touching, mutual and self-masturbation, oral sex and intercourse by a child, not involving an adult.

○ **Gross Assault:** Grossly obscene pictures of sexual assault, involving penetrative sex, masturbation or oral sex involving an adult.

Child pornography offenses are valid diagnostic indicator of Pedophilia.

○ **Sadistic:** Pictures showing a child being tied, bound, beaten, whipped or otherwise subject to something that implies pain as well as pictures where an animal is involved in some form of sexual behaviour with a child.

How Pedophiles Trap Children

(a) Pedophiles use false identity to trap the children/teenagers.

(b) Pedophiles contact children/teens in various chat rooms which are used by children/teen to interact with other children/teen.

(c) Befriend the child/teen.

(d) Extract personal information from the child/teen by winning his confidence.

(e) Get the e-mail address of the child/teen and start making contacts on victim's e-mail id.

(f) Starts sending pornographic images/text to the victim including child pornographic images in order to help child/teen shed his inhibitions so that a feeling is created in the mind of the victim that what is being fed to him is normal and that everybody does it.

(g) Extract personal information from child/teen.

(h) At the end of it, the pedophiles set up a meeting with the child/teen out of the house and then drag him into the net to further sexually assault him or to use him as a sex object.

Internet Safety Tips for Children

1. Do not give out identifying information such as name, home address, school name or telephone number in a chat room.

2. Do not send your photograph to any one on the Internet without initially checking with the parent or guardian.

3. Do not respond to messages or bulletin board items that are obscene, belligerent or threatening.

4. Never arrange a face-to-face meeting without informing your parent or guardian.

Putting personal data on net is like giving your whereabouts to strangers.

5. Remember that people online may not be who they seem to be.

Strategies to Rid Your Community from Pornography

Pornography's power to undermine individual and social functioning is powerful and deep. Pornography hurts adults, children, couples, families and society. It is immoral to treat women as objects for sale and for use and abuse. Women are not just playthings. No society that tolerates – let alone condones or promotes – the selective abuse of women and children can call itself good.

Zero tolerance for pornography is required to make your locality no-porn zone.

Social scientists, clinical psychologists, and biologists have begun to clarify some of the social and psychological effects of pornography, and neurologists are beginning to delineate the biological mechanisms through which pornography produces its powerful effects on people. The fundamental role of government (including the courts) is to protect innocent citizens, most especially children and adolescents, and to protect the sound functioning of the basic institutions of family, church, school and marketplace. Our present and future families need protection from this insidious enemy of love, affection, and of family and social stability. The silence and apathy of the community toward pornography must end. We must speak out. Our society has suffered too much already because of our silence on pornography.

Why Porn is Dangerous?

- The habitual consumption of pornography can result in a diminished satisfaction with mild forms of pornography and a correspondingly strong desire for more deviant and violent material.
- Exposure to pornography frequently results in sexual illnesses, unplanned pregnancies, and sexual addiction.
- Exposure to pornography may incite children to act out sexually against other children.
- Pornography increases sexual callousness toward women and trivialize rape.

Harmful Effects of Pornography

Effects on individual: Pornography significantly distorts attitudes and perceptions about the nature of sexual intercourse. Men who habitually look at pornography have a higher tolerance for abnormal sexual behaviors, sexual aggression, promiscuity, and even rape.

Internet porn is changing our sexual attitude affecting health and conjugal relation.

Effects on married life: Married men who are involved in pornography feel less satisfied with their conjugal relations and less emotionally attached to their wives. It is a major threat to marriage, to family, to children, and to individual happiness. Pornographic use may lead to infidelity and even divorce.

Effects on children: Pornography viewing among teenagers disorients them during that developmental phase when they have to learn how to handle their sexuality and when they are most vulnerable to uncertainty about their sexual beliefs and moral values. Adolescents who view pornography feel shame, diminished self-confidence, and sexual uncertainty.

Effects on society: The presence of sexually oriented businesses significantly harms the surrounding community, leading to increases in crime and decreases in property values. Child sex-offenders, for example, are often involved not only in the viewing, but also in the distribution, of pornography.

Why We Must Rid Our Community of Pornography

Sexually oriented businesses (SOBs) – pornography stores and strip clubs – deleteriously affect their surrounding communities. For instance, SOBs along Garden Grove Boulevard in California contributed to 36 percent of all crime in that area. A similar study in Centralia, Washington, found that, after an SOB opened, the serious crime rate rose significantly in the vicinity of the SOB's address. Findings such as these generally come from studies commissioned by cities to measure the incidence of the eight serious crimes of the Uniform Crime Reports: homicide, rape, assault, robbery, burglary, theft, auto theft and arson.

SOBs have been found to cause more crime than non-sexually oriented nightclubs and bars. A report from Daytona Beach, Florida, found that SOB neighborhoods have 270 percent more total crime than non-SOB control neighborhoods and 180 percent more than non-SOB neighborhoods with "taverns." A study in Adams County, Colorado, found that 83 percent of crimes in a neighborhood featuring two adult businesses were connected to those adult businesses.

A study of SOBs in Phoenix, Arizona, found that the number of sex offenses was 506 percent greater in a neighborhood containing a SOB. Sexual deviants are attracted to these areas, intending to pay for sexual pleasures. The forbidden partners they desire include children, the invalid, and the elderly.

Tips for Safeguarding Your Children Online

While online computer exploration opens a world of possibilities for young people, expanding their horizons and exposing them to different cultures and ways of life, they can be exposed to dangers as they explore the information highway. There are individuals who attempt to sexually exploit children through the use of online services and the Internet. The following is a list of helpful tips to protect your family.

Parents and kids can jointly explore safe and transparent ways to use technology.

1. Develop a trusting relationship with your child early and keep the door of communication open.

2. If you have reason to suspect your child is viewing inappropriate sites, do not overact – approach your son or daughter with respect.

3. Know your children's online friends.

4. Check CDs, pen drives and zip disks and online History Files.

5. Get to know and use the parental controls provided by your Internet Service Provider and/ or blocking software.

6. Tell your child to NEVER give out identifying information such as name, address, school name or telephone number to people on the Internet.

7. Teach your child about responsible use of the resources on the Internet. Instruct your child to NEVER arrange face-to-face meetings with someone he/she met online and NOT to respond to messages or bulletin board postings that are suggestive, obscene, belligerent or harassing.

8. Explain to your child to NEVER post pictures of him/her on the Internet.

Steps to Free Your Locality of Pornography:

1. Take a vocal stand against soft core pornography. The road to high community standards begins with a strong message that soft core pornography is unacceptable.

2. If you notice any erotic activity in cyber café, bars, or find obscene material in your locality, you must write a letter or call and report to your local law enforcement agency. It's reported in the same manner you would report any other crime.

Consider yourself as first person to rid your community of pornography.

3. Many general video rental stores contain a section with "adult" material. If the store rents or sells material that is obscene under a state statute, the store can be prosecuted. Children are accidently exposed to adult materials and weakens the community standards.

4. Organise pornographic awareness meet at any public place involving community members, leaders and officials and raise the issue of wide impact of pornography on society. Aware the participants about devastating effects of pornography and its impact on your community.

5. Suggest parents, schools, cyber cafes and service providers to provide filtered Internet service to protect your community from harmful effects of pornography.

6. Boycott distributors of pornography and let them know why. Support retailers who make a commitment to the family by not selling pornography.

7. Encourage municipal and county officials to adopt and enforce strict local zoning ordinances designed to regulate sexually oriented businesses.

8. Form anti-porn group to help protect as many as we can and take as many with us as we can, to free your locality of pornography.

9. If all attempts to eradicate porn business fail, then organize youth rally to aware every citizen about poisonous effects of pornography on children. Ask every person in the locality to take part in the movement and ensure creation of a porn-free society.

Source: A Guide To What One Person Can Do About Pornography, American Family Association, Inc.

Scriptures and holy books are like teachers who impart life-transforming teachings without canning or admonition.
– Pt Sriram Sharma Acharya

PART III
THE UNIQUE ART OF LIFE MANAGEMENT

Entertainment is essential in today's life as a means of mental rejuvenation and stress relief. The nature of human mind is such that it always needs and aspires for joy, irrespective of method or money invested these recreational activities. People do have different tastes for entertainment, but in some form or the other, it usually relates to some sort of sensual pleasure like joys of taste, fragrance, melody, sight of beauty etc. Some like outdoor games, tourism, gardening, reading and writing while others

Real entertainment imparts happiness, peace and tranquility.

prefer listening to music, watching movies, games or simply chatting. Pleasures of sense organs set the basis of its amusement. People link entertainment with enjoyment; however with creative diversion, one can turn its cheerful effects into additional benefits of efficient management of life. At a superficial level, entertainment is an act, event, or performance designed to achieve pleasure and relaxation. But do we get the real joy out of these activities? Do we reap any long-term benefit or lasting happiness from these recreational activities?

Entertainment for Momentary Delight!

People eat or drink anything that gives temporary stimulation to tongue. Some are crazy for fried stuff while some others for cheese-full, buttery softness and others crave for lavish sweets. Increased greed of the tongue and burning of health and money are certain here rather than attaining any real joy. Similar is the case with watching movies, colourful paintings, photographs, fireworks etc. Considering the cost and time consumed and momentary excitation felt, would anyone get same feeling again and again? In general, humorous company, good musicians, singers, dancers, and actors provide immediate entertainment. Lighter chat with people around us is also not possible all the time. Many people enjoy relaxing idly. They eagerly await for vacations and find excuses. Work appears burden for them. Thus, it is in the fitness of things to realize the psychological basis of entertainment and look for the nearest and always accessible mode of that would serve the purpose of entertainment.

Essence of Entertainment

Prime difference between inanimate and animate world is activity. Physical activity is necessary for maintaining good health. Physically handicapped persons are also taught special exercises for adept blood circulation. Mental activity is no less important. Empty mind becomes a devil's workshop. Untoward thoughts, haphazard imaginations and negative

Exploring nature's beauty imparts real joy and happiness.

tendencies accumulate faster in an idle mind. Emotions also play significant role in deciding our mental state. Adversities, arrogance and obsessions bring inevitable stress in life. The irony is that one adopts artificial and unmindful means of entertainment to get rid of these stresses, which fuel more mental and physical weaknesses. The light of bliss, the music of entertainment lies in your own self. Any activity, interaction or experience becomes entertainment if you feel the pulse of joy in it. It is the individual self that feels joy and happiness through different sense organs. Thus, by changing our attitude and interest, we can develop spirit of entertainment in daily chores too.

Erotic Entertainment

Driven by sensuous lust, some people find amusement in erotic thinking, imagination, watching pornography and other sexual activities by the means of novels, magazines, poetry and paintings. The fire of sensuous lust inflames higher with every such act. People addicted to such amusements are often found dissatisfied, easily irritable and short-tempered. It penetrates in the mind of the viewer and compels him to invest more time and money in achieving satisfaction. The excessive thoughts about sex would quite often impact routine work and mental concentration. This kind of pleasure diminishes their potentials of deep and focused thinking and creates mental infirmity, perversion, or even psychopathic mentality. Erotic thinking and sensuous orgasm negatively affects hormonal secretion. It triggers release of psychotropic chemicals in blood stream resulting in stimulation of pleasure centers of brain. As a result, brain produces obsessive compulsive behaviour to relive the pleasurable sensations.

Experiencing Quality Entertainment

○ **Orderliness:** In our own routine, working style, at home or work places, we can transform filth into cleanliness, disorder into order and lethargy into meaningful activity. Attempting to be a more organised person and orderly management of things is a wonderful way of creative entertainment. Arranging things on the working table or at home itself gives a positive diversion to the mind.

○ **Reading:** Most of us read newspapers, magazines or storybooks in casual way and spend some extra time. However, good books are permanent source of inspiration that enlightens reader with positive and virtuous thoughts and inspire one towards good deeds and excellence. There might be lack of virtuous talents in our surroundings but there is no scarcity of inspiring narrations, works of art revolving round noble characters or commentaries. Reading or listening to these is indeed an enchanting source that would entertain and illuminate your mind.

○ **Interaction with family and friends:** Rather than killing time in gossiping and watching television, it is better to spend some free time with your well wishers. Sitting with family members, playing with children, reading storybooks for them, sharing knowledge, positive thoughts and experiences would not only provide relief from day-to-day stress but also impart guidance to others. Try some creative work on holidays collectively with family and friends. Your daily chores, routine job would then become more interesting.

○ **Playing with children:** We all see and meet children in our families and neighbourhood. All young children are cute and lovable. God has gifted us with living toys all around in the form of children. Their company is such a wonderful mode of calming and rejuvenating the mind. If our heart is soft, the company of a child will have soothing and inspiring effects on our emotions. Anyone in their company can receive love, soft touch and joy.

○ **Music – the universal entertainment:** Music provides the best way to express emotions. Whenever we listen to music, our limbs begin to oscillate with its melody. This shows that our inner sense has got an intimate relationship with music. Melodious music offers instant relief from physical and mental agony. While the refined, sonorous, and devotional music may transmute an ordinary personality into a divinely refined one, the erotic and exciting music could decline one's mental and emotional heights upside down. Music should be inspiring and create an environment for emotional enlightenment, in-depth peace and tranquillity for listeners.

There are two ways to lead a happy life – minimise your need and live in harmony with the circumstances.
— *Pt. Sriram Sharma Acharya*

Music: The Nectar of Life

Screeching parrots, tinkling of the beetles, singing of nightingale or the grumbling of a frog – each produces a unique natural rhythm and forms magical world of music. Most of the animals have specific 'Musical' voice to convey messages. Whenever we listen to music, our limbs begin to oscillate with its melody. This shows that our inner sense has got an intimate relationship with music. Increase in body's energy-level after performing or attending a musical concert or a dance program are common examples of physical effects of music. Music provides the best way to express emotions. Melodious music offers instant relief from physical and mental agony. While the refined, sonorous, and devotional music may transmute an ordinary personality into a divinely refined one, the erotic and exciting music could decline one's mental and emotional heights upside down. Music should be inspiring and create an environment for emotional enlightenment, in-depth peace and tranquility for listeners.

Calming Effects of Music

Researchers have found that music does affect physiological system of every creature. Soothing music has also been found to help animals reduce their stress and causes behavioral modification. In birds, three times larger length of the vocal cord in the males as compared with females is attributed to the frequent use of amplitudes of the voice to express feelings of love, anger, jealous, and joy. Snake charmers hypnotize poisonous snakes by playing the wind instrument. They start dancing on the tune of the musical instrument. Studies have also revealed that when cats are exposed to classical music, they calm down faster.

Scientific Facts of Music

- Music can help reduce chronic pain by more than 20% and alleviate depression
- Music causes the body to release endorphins which reduces pain
- Music stimulates release of antibody Immunoglobulin A and boosts immunity
- Music slows down breathing and heart beat and improves motor coordination

Do You Know?

Albert Einstein developed the passion for music at an early age. He was good at playing violin. The music of Mozart and Bach was his favorite. Einstein himself says that the reason he was so smart is because he always loved to play violin.

Music Activates Brain!

Melodic Intonation Therapy (MIT) is a therapeutic process used by music therapists to help patients with communication disorder, which is associated with brain's left hemisphere. Positron emission tomography (PET) scans have revealed that the left hemisphere was reactivated by the end of MIT resulting in significant changes in brain structure. Also, right-hemisphere axon connections in patients were found to be increased in volume after MIT. Many doctors are now prescribing music to help treat patients with diseases like Parkinson's, Alzheimer's, and people with anxiety and depression.

Music on the mind

When we listen to music, it's processed in many different areas of our brain. The extent of the brain's involvement was scarcely imagined until the early nineties, when functional brain imaging became possible. The major computational centres include:

CORPUS CALLOSUM ⊃
Connects left and right hemispheres.

MOTOR CORTEX ⊃
Movement, foot tapping, dancing, and playing an instrument.

PREFRONTAL CORTEX ⊃
Creation of expectations, violation and satisfactioin of expectations.

NUCLEUS ACCUMBENS ⊃
Emotional reactions to music.

AMYGDALA ⊃
Emotional reactions to music.

C SENSORY CORTEX
Tactile feedback from playing an instument and dancing.

C AUDITORY CORTEX
The first stages of listening to sounds. The perception and analysis of tones.

C HIPPOCAMPUS
Memory for music, musical experiences and contexts.

C VISUAL CORTEX
Reading music, looking at a performer's or one's own movements.

C CEREBELLUM
Movement such as foot tapping, dancing, and playing an instrument. Also involved in emotional reactions to music.

MIKE FAILLE/THE GLOBE AND MAIL ✖ SOURCE: THIS IS YOUR BRAIN ON MUSIC: THE SCIENCE OF A HUMAN OBSESSION

Restraining Sensual Lust and Desires

Some audacious youths regard discipline of senses as a barrier against their enthusiasm and energy; they want to break all mental, social and national norms. Truth is that you cannot enjoy the pleasure of senses for long without observing self-restrain. The musical instrument Sitar produces melodious music only if its wires are controlled carefully. Just think of the fate of the horse-rider who cannot hold the bridle of the horse. Appropriate control over horse is a must if

Love is sacrifice but stay for long time; Lust is sensation and ends quickly.

the rider wants to reach some-where safely. Similarly, prudent vigil and self-discipline are essential for progress, peace and happiness. The dignity of human life lies in uprooting the beastly tendencies, winning over the passions and rising for higher goals. You should be the master and not a slave of your body and mind. A wise man rules over his sense organs and makes constructive use of them as per the directions of wisdom.

Animals' Unique Sexual Behaviour

How fruitful a controlled sexual life is, can be learnt from a variety of example available in the nature. A large number of members of the animal kingdom demonstrate such a remarkable degree of discipline and responsibility in matters associated with reproduction and its consequent events, that one finds them certainly better than the 'social animal' of today. Similar examples of patience, sincerity, fidelity and industrious sharing of responsibilities are found in the families of kiwi, penguins, emu, ostrich etc. Even the tiny creatures like the ants are ahead of many higher organisms in the regard. Why cannot all the men as 'husbands' also offer harmonious co-operation to their wives, especially in the societies where the letter are expected to strictly follow the doctrines of virtuous, dutiful life with a due fidelity towards their husbands?

Sex and Vital Energy

The brain and the genitals are two vital sources of energy in the human body. The genital organ is empowered with bio-electrical and bio-magnetic energy, its proper functioning is responsible for the normal maintenance of body function. Similarly, the brain controls the nervous system. A healthy state and balanced utilization of both together is essential for metabolism and various psychological functions. The subtle energy centre in genital organ is the source of youthfulness, charm activity and longevity. Over stimulation of the sex organs should be avoided maximally in order to maintain the neural powers of body.

Biological contact between the two sexes involve the flow of their mutual vital energies from higher level to the lower ones thus, the sexual intercourse amounts to the lowering of the mental and spiritual abilities of the better partner in the pair. People with strong will power and extra ordinary mental faculties should be more careful about preserving their vital energies, because they are likely to lose them by transmitting them to their counter parts during sexual intercourse. Under no circumstance should a sexual contact occur without the willingness of both the partners. In married life, practicing purity of thoughts and feelings, mutual trust and friendly cooperation, with healthy humour and entertainment are necessary for the nurturing of love and affection between the life partners.

Sexual excitation or erotic feelings are likely to attack everyone in today's indiscipline and morally polluted atmosphere. Any kind of imbalance in this activity affects the nervous system negatively. Obvious consequences of this loss include reduction in brilliance, memory power, intelligence, liveliness, firmness of mind, immunity and physical abilities of body.

Redirecting Sensual Lust

Sexual desire is a natural function of the living system. If suppressed, it would, as per the universal law of action and reaction, result in harmful negative effects or become more aggressive. An easy, natural and scientifically justified way out is that of avoiding the occasions of sensual and mental excitations and diverting the mind towards creative entertainment. Bodily lusts when they raise their heads in time, appear very pleasing, but their fruits are so unbearable, that a solution becomes almost impossible. Lust, violence during sexual excitation and the hideous crimes like rape illustrate the destructive effects of sex, which arise due to the unethical, uncontrolled, immoral and erotic thinking. On contrary, the constructive power of sex is most commonly manifested in the reproduction of an offspring. The control and optimal utilization of the vital power of sex can be compared with the setting up of a reservoir for rain water and utilizing it for irrigation purpose. This latent power may also be utilized in augmenting mental concentration which is necessary for the development of one's intellectual faculties.

Love verses Lust

Eternal love is a divine virtue, a preeminent source of auspicious peace and joy. It purifies the mind, wanes out vices of mind and generates soothing sentiments and enthusiasm. Hearty, healthy and prosperous life is an obvious byproduct of these benefits. It is the deep sentiment of love that induces patience, courage and tolerance in a person. It is because of immense love for child that a mother sacrifices her

Love always resides in heart; your beloved only touches feelings at right time.

own health and comforts and bears all pains of pregnancy. No resource of luxury and pleasure would make you happy if there is no place for love in your lives. On the contrary, lust is a selfish means to fulfill sexual desire which lasts for few minutes. People commit a mighty mistake to think that till they are youthful, body is full of vigour and virility then why not luxuriate and enjoy the pleasure of sex. Instead of that they should think that till they are young, body has strength and capacity then why not take measures to defeat this enemy. Times ahead when old age will come, this immortal enemy will be difficult to die.

Tender emotions are the pivot of *jivana sadhana*. All the virtues in life flow from and revolve around them. It is emotions that give the sense of contentment in life. Whatever new heights of development and progress are scaled in disregard of emotions will leave a nagging feeling of emptiness and vacuity. All the acquisitions of wealth, power, respect and honour fail to give inner satisfaction; the interior always feels thirsty for something else. The origin of all psychological ailments lies in hidden, crushed, betrayed and tormented emotions. On the other hand, if there is a proper sprouting of emotions in life and they are nurtured with care and love, miraculous changes are inevitable. Such persons become masters of innumerable virtues and the fragrance of their personalities permeates the whole surrounding.

Do You Know?

- Love and sexual thought influences creativity and concrete thinking because they are associated with devotion, commitment and intimacy.
- True love relieves stress and pain. Oxytocin, the so-called love or cuddle hormone, is produced during an embrace, holding arms or cuddle.

Redirecting Sensual Lust

Sexual desire is a natural function of the living system. If suppressed, it would, as per the universal law of action and reaction, result in harmful negative effects or become more aggressive. An easy, natural and scientifically justified way out is that of avoiding the occasions of sensual and mental excitations and diverting the mind towards creative entertainment. Bodily lusts when they raise their heads in time, appear very pleasing, but their fruits are so unbearable, that a solution becomes almost impossible. Lust, violence during sexual excitation and the hideous crimes like rape illustrate the destructive effects of sex, which arise due to the unethical, uncontrolled, immoral and erotic thinking. On contrary, the constructive power of sex is most commonly manifested in the reproduction of an offspring. The control and optimal utilization of the vital power of sex can be compared with the setting up of a reservoir for rain water and utilizing it for irrigation purpose. This latent power may also be utilized in augmenting mental concentration which is necessary for the development of one's intellectual faculties.

Steps to Control Sexual Desire

○ **Keep Faith in Your Efforts:** You must take the problem of uncontrolled sexual excitation seriously and consider it as other weaknesses of human being with confidence on positive outcomes of your effort to control sensual lust.

○ **Stop Tempting Yourself:** Avoid circumstances which arouse sensual feeling such as watching pornography, reading erotic literature, lustful thoughts and touching private parts etc. Keep yourself busy in creative works.

○ **Avoid Close Contact:** Always try to maintain some physical distance with friends of opposite sex and avoid touching his/her body during interactions.

○ **Control Your Eyes:** Try to keep your eyes away from teenagers walking down the street in high skirts, tight clothes, and follow the practice of bouncing your eyes.

○ **Seek Spiritual Guidance:** Spiritual practices and reading spiritual books boost inner strength and provide mental strength to fight sexual temptation. Also seek advice from nearest spiritual advisor without hesitation.

When you love someone, you love the person as they are, and not as you would like them to be.

—*Leo Tolstoy*

What is 'True' Love?

The words of a holy seer, **Swami Ramtirtha**, are very enlightening in this context. His personality, a confluence of tapa, wisdom and love, had acquired a divine magnetism. Countless number of people rushed to him in distress and returned with a smile. One day a woman came to him, she was a picture of gloom and despondence. Someone had sent her to *Swamiji*. She had come somehow, but was unable to speak anything. Deep depression had made her tongue-tied. For a long moment, she remained sitting like a statue, saying nothing. **Swami Ramtirtha** too said nothing to her; only kept gazing at her with compassion and empathy that melted the ice of accumulated pain. She kept weeping and **Ramtirtha** kept looking at her with affection. The panacea of love and understanding gradually enable her to regain her voice. With tears in her eyes, she narrated her story about how after sacrificing everything – money, body, mind, life – she had been betrayed and had got only dejection in return.

After patiently listening to her, **Ramtirtha** spoke somberly: "Sister, everyone in this world behaves according to the level of his capability. One's physical, mental, intellectual and emotional capacities bound and circumscribe him and limit his conduct to the available measure. Those whose emotions are soiled in selfishness and venality are only worthy of forgiveness. Very helpless are these poor souls". "It is impossible, in that case, to get true love in life"? The woman asked. "No, it is not so, "**Swami Ramtirtha** replied, "True love comes, but only to those who know how to love truly". "My love was also true", the visitor remonstrated. "No sister, your love had expectation. Also, there was a poisonous element of lust dissolved in it, whereas true love appears only in the form of selfless service, compassion and reverential faith."

The woman realized the essence of **Ramtirtha's** words. She now knew that love is only given; it does not demand anything. Love is the name of unconditional giving. It is the name of emotions that are free of lust, longing and egoity. Having assimilated this wisdom, she joined a hospital as a nurse. Her emotions found an outlet in selfless service.

Respect Women's Dignity

Although the status of women has been uplifted in the recent past, with the advent of educational and scientific development in several parts of the world, much still remain to be done in this direction. Latent propagation of eroticism in the of modernity, art, entertainment and humour continue to degrade femininity in general; suppression of women by their one relatives in the name of religious or social discipline still show its presence in many part of the society; the economical, social and political disparities between the two sex still persist.

Great Persons' Respect for Women

Prophet Mohammad: My heaven lies beneath the feet of my mother.

Saint William: In woman's eyes, God has provided two lamps, so that men who have lost their way can in their light, find it again.

Mahatma Gandhi: Man can never be a woman's equal in the spirit of selfless service with which nature has endowed her.

Malala Yousafzai: I raise up my voice—not so I can shout, but so that those without a voice can be heard...we cannot succeed when half of us are held back.

Oprah Winfrey: I finally realized that being grateful to my body was key to giving more love to myself.

Woman is not an object of lust but cause of your existence in the world.

Dr. A.P.J. Abdul Kalam: Empowerment of women is essential as their value system leads to the development of a good family, society and ultimately a good nation.

Kofi Annan: There is no tool for development more effective than empowerment of woman.

Unknown: The willingness to listen, the patience to understand, the strength to support, the heart to care and just be there; that is the beauty of a woman.

Unknown: It is hard to be a woman. You must think like a man, act like a lady, look like a young girl, and work like a horse.

20 Stepping Stone to Success: Character Building

Character is the unification of a person's attributes, traits and abilities inspired by virtuous thoughts and actions. Character is expressed by doing the right thing for the right reason even when no one is watching. The people, who keep their unbridled desires in control and transform them into virtuous actions, are considered as person of ethical strength or noble character. The piousness in action, behaviour, thoughts and emotions

Noble thoughts and unconditional love create foundation of good character.

glorifies the life. Your character is shaped according to your thought, desire, wish and conduct. Building good character is all about addition, not subtraction. It is the process of addition in your life that brings the character. In so doing, you automatically take care of the other negative aspects. We add honesty, compassion, altruism, generosity, sacrifice, courtesy, and prudent behaviour to make good character.

You Only Pose Power to Build Character

We ourselves have to make efforts to inculcate virtues, righteousness and chastity in ourselves. Parents, teachers and the society could definitely guide us, but we have to move on this path alone. We should follow self-restraint and accomplish spiritual pursuits to practice morality. Wicked elements of the society would oppose us, but we should neither worry about it nor should we pay attention to what people say. Whatever may be the circumstances, we should face them boldly. Man is not slave of the circumstances, he is their creator, controller and master. He who could maintain his honesty, courage, and patience even amongst adversities is the real champion.

"A noble person is humble like the poor in riches and prosperity; and generous like the rich in adversity."

— *Pt. Sriram Sharma Acharya*

Declining Character, Rising Wealth

Character is the most precious strength and possession of man. A person without moral strength, if obtains wealth, will soon ruin all his assets in enjoyment and lavish lifestyle. If he is learned, will utilise his knowledge in conspiracy, cheating, and deceiving, and if he is powerful, will commit atrocities. Such wealth, wisdom, and power being controlled by characterless person are fatal for society. In modern time, there has been a spurt in our assets, credibility, education etc. but proportionately our character is declining.

If you want to give something special, give courage to a hopeless person.

Increasing maliciousness like depravation, dishonesty, deceit, partiality, jealousy, is the repercussion of covetousness. Lacking character causes degeneration of strength, prosperity, and progress. A society comprising of the people having high moral standards adds to their repute. People accord great respect to such person and he is trusted for his words. The prowess of leadership and inspiring the society can be attained only by high virtual character.

Become Your Own Master

From children to elders, everyone commits mistake. When others commit mistake, we soon get angry and want to punish them immediately. On the other hand, we keep hiding our own faults and try every possible way to prevent the punishment. This is the reason why we keep committing the mistakes and eventually get used to them. If you commit a mistake, don't waste time feeling regretful or guilty. We should develop the habit of punishing ourselves for our mistakes and not wait for someone else to punish us. The punishment could be as simple as skipping the meal or scolding ourselves for the foolishness depending upon gravity of mistake. Encourage and reward your mind for every success in this attempt. Ponder over the benefits of good and refined habits. Soon you will realize rise in self-confidence, moral conduct and self-satisfaction which form the foundation of noble character.

"Try not to become a man of success, but rather try to become a man of value" — *Albert Einstein*

Components of Good Character

1. **Honesty:** Honesty simply implies authentic transactions of goods and money. However, domain of honesty is not limited to business only. Money spent in extravagancy and profligate lifestyle incurs unnecessary expenses that compel to retrieve money by unfair means. Anything which is not earned by steady efforts is a dishonest earning such as gambling, theft, lottery etc. This should be remembered that only honest person can attain self-respect, affection and cooperation. Even dishonest person expects his servant to be honest. This clearly upholds how important is the might and need of honesty.

2. **Modesty:** A great person has said, 'Modesty is priceless, but it can buy anything.' Modesty plays a vital role in attaining success along with self-respect and social prestige. Manifestation of modesty and ethics is the sign of civility. There is sudden upsurge of friends and aids of the modest person while the close ones of unethical person start maintaining distance with him. Everyone should practice modesty not only to elders but to younger ones also with same temperament.

3. **Self-dependence:** Relying on self is such a mighty trait that it invokes courage, commitment and ability to carry out any work. So long you depend on others for resolution of problems, you are in deception. It is said that man makes his own destiny. If you want wealth, intellect, strength and wisdom then inculcate courage and skills. Start increasing your talent matching your ambitions. Every person has got ample autonomy to rise above the common stage and there is no reason you cannot succeed.

4. **Sexual Abstinence:** Sexuality is not an instrument of pleasure. The body uses the same energy and material wasted through sexual activity to heal itself. A true celibate possesses high energy, a sharp brain, gigantic will-power, bold understanding, and retentive memory. Those who have not observed the vow of celibacy become slaves of anger, laziness and fear. Physical abstinence is the first step but mental celibacy is the real celibacy. By restraining yourself physically and letting the mind run wild you will only be cheating yourself. The secret of health lies in preservation of this vital force. He who wastes this vital and precious energy cannot have physical, mental, moral and spiritual development.

Continence Improves Brain Power

There is a remarkable similarity of chemical composition between the semen and the central nervous system, both being especially rich in lecithin, cholesterin and phosphorus compounds, which would indicate that seminal emissions withdraw from the body substances necessary for the nutrition of nervous tissues. Excessive involuntary seminal losses are debilitating to the nervous system and may cause neurasthenia. Continence is beneficial to the brain (for conserved lecithin from retained semen is a true brain food).

Easy Steps to Improve Character

○ Choose a set of rules, morals, or principles that you believe will lead to a happy, satisfying, and righteous life, and a better world.

○ Sexual desire is natural urge of everybody and in certain limits, it is beneficial for health but sometimes, it becomes out of control. Sexual thoughts overpower mind leading to immoral acts or practices. Try to avoid thinking about or seeing the opposite sex as far as possible.

A man's conduct is true measure of his character.

○ Subscribe to the ethics of a particular religion, develop practice of reading inspiring books, novels and seek spiritual guidance from an expert.

○ Be conscious every day of the decisions you make, however big or small. Try to avoid thinking about or seeing the opposite sex as far as possible. Do not bother if honesty gives you immediate pain but always give priority to self-satisfaction and long-term gain rather than popular route.

○ Do not make just anybody your ideal in life. Restrain from copying deeds of unethical person. Be conscious in selecting any new habit, thought or conduct.

○ Good habits make good character. The character required to attain eternal life must be formed in this life with good habits supplying the building material. We should become so involved in acquiring good quality traits and participating in character-building activities that there is no time to engage in anything worthless or harmful.

Do You Know?

When Mother Teresa went to a bakery man for bread for her orphan children. As she raised her arms, the bakery man just spit on her hand. Then Mother Teresa told him, I would keep this for me, but give me some bread for my children while holding her another hand. On that spot, the bakery man realized Mother Teresa's gentleness and become a main bread donor for her orphanage.

"We sow our thoughts, and we reap our actions; we sow our actions, and we reap our habits; we sow our habits, and we reap our characters; we sow our characters, and we reap our destiny."
— (C. A. Hall, *The Home Book of Quotations*, New York: Dodd, Mead & Company, 1935, p. 845.)

---

21 Fundamental Tenets of Married Life

Every man is in his natural, normal state is incomplete. To overcome this incompleteness, he joins hands with another power to proceed from the state of incompleteness to completeness. Association of man and woman has a very natural, important and useful purpose. In normal course, this is willingly accepted by almost all adult men and women through the institution of marriage. However, in the recent past, many distortions and dissatisfaction have gradually crept into the married life. As a result, couples do not find the desired satisfaction in family life, begin

Your family is the most precious gift of God.

to find fault with the institution of marriage and often treat it as a burden. Many prefer keeping off from it because of fear of responsibilities or deluded religious conceptions. Creating and raising a happy family is in fact a very natural, important path of self-development. In this process, self expands from a single individual into two as husband-wife, then with a child into three and then into relatives, neighbours, society, region, state and nation. Thus, the entire humanity gradually begins to embrace one's sphere of own self.

Happiness in Limited Means of Income

It is incorrect to worry about how the requirements of all people in the family be met when the income is less. If income is less, then it is necessary to make the lifestyle simple and frugal. If coarse cloths and less expensive food grains used, way of life is kept simple and undesirable items of show off and fashion are voluntarily and happily renounced, then all can live happily in limited resources. This world has many rich people who live luxurious lives, who show off their wealth and indulge in sensual pleasures. There is no wisdom in copying rich, extravagant, fashionable and ostentatious people. Instead we must try to copy their sharp intellect, smartness, hard work, if any, and alacrity. The time that is wasted in useless act can be used to keep home, cloths and body clean and tidy. Simplicity and poverty are no hindrances to maintain peace and happiness in family life.

Top Four Requirements for Happiness in Family

The First Requirement: Good Health

All in the family must get uniform opportunity towards good health, education, entertainment and building a bright future. Health actually gets spoilt due to disorganized way of life. Any kind of expensive, exotic food cannot mitigate the harm caused by improper lifestyle. If we pay full attention towards sufficient food, sound sleep and regular exercises, excretion, bathing and cleanliness etc then we can easily keep ourselves from falling ill. It is prudent to fight common elements by

If you can't love your partner, make him a true friend in all respect.

fasting, eating fresh fruits and mild vegetable soups. We can fight with the ailment by taking advice of some experienced noble person and using simple basic medicines and helping the patient follow necessary health-discipline.

The Second Requirement: Good Education

Just as food is necessary to overcome hunger, education is necessary to nurture the mind. Every member of the family must be provided good education. They must be provided thoughtfully chosen books that help them in furthering knowledge about topics like human body, mind, social issues, religion and so on. All must be able to understand the problems of life and read opinions of genuine and sagacious on these issues. At the same time through methods like debates, questioning, reasoning, listening to discourses on important topics one should enhance one's information, intelligence and analytical capability.

The Third Requirement: Healthy Entertainment

If man does not get an opportunity to enjoy, to laugh, play and amuse himself, then his mental state would turn acrid, irritable, intolerant and pessimistic. Such people become very suspecting and remain dissatisfied with the world. Surely, entertainment is a necessary nutrition without which life begins to wither. But, one must always try to save oneself from entertainment that gives only sensual pleasures, is unhealthy, in bad taste and vulgar. Through soothing music, singing, playing instruments, traveling, meeting people, dining with friends, visiting fairs and carnivals and many such ways, we can occupy ourselves in healthy entertainment.

The Fourth Requirement: Opportunity to Grow

We must never get satisfied if the needs of everyone in the family is being somehow met today. Instead, we must plan as to how the future of each and every member of our family can become bright, happy, prosperous and inspirational to others. It is necessary to always think of ways and to continuously put in efforts to refine and elevate ours as well as others' lives higher and even higher. We must continuously work on plans that help in the development of both internal and external aspects of life. It is also necessary to make everyone capable of earning one's own living. Till sufficient education, qualification and experience is attained to solve mental, economic and social problems, life cannot become happy.

A Troubleshooting Exercise

If we manage to make our family members righteous and truthful by our efforts, goodwill and sacrifice, then this high quality deed of ours would not be inferior to any other benevolent deed in the world. We must keep examining very carefully the following facts. Is every man, women, or child in the family getting sufficient opportunity for the growth of their physical and mental faculties? Is anyone being denied his/her natural right to grow in life and create a bright future? Is anyone getting undue luxuries and pampering and is anyone else being unfairly pressurized and oppressed? When observed minutely, answers to these questions can clearly point to where there is a need to improve the organization of the family. All the activities done for the family must be divided into these categories and then ideas to correct the errors made must be found out.

1. Searching for mistakes and errors;
2. Accepting them;
3. Being ashamed of them, and
4. Putting sincere and honest efforts to correct them — whoever likes this process and adopts it in his life, his mistakes reduce day-by-day and soon he rids himself off all his weaknesses.

Quick Fact

Mr. Karam Chand and Mrs Kartari Chand from England married on 11 December 1925, is the longest living married couple in world.

Secrets of Happy Family Life

1. **Create Positive Environment:** The main reason for increase in strife in families is 'unwarranted reservations.' We usually mix very well and converse openly with outsiders, but remain reserved with our family members and talk to them very little. The essential reasons for encouraging conduct like respect and regard for elders of family, and decency, modesty, tolerance, etc have been forgotten, and highly distorted forms of customs now prevail in the families.

Married life is an institution where one learns unconditional love and sacrifice.

2. **Self-Governance:** If a decision has to be taken in the family, opinion of all men and women must be considered. Members of a family should not feel that someone's dictate is being enforced upon them. All the work should be distributed evenly among each family member. Except for special circumstances, all in the family must eat same food, and wear clothes and hold all possessions uniformly. Whichever family adopts these principle remains happy and contented.

3. **Avoid Misunderstandings:** Members of a family should follow some rules to avoid clashes and misunderstandings. Elders of the family must not demand excessive courtesy from the younger generation. They must treat them with generosity, love, sympathy and forgiveness. If someone makes a mistake, then in solitude he/she must be tenderly explained the harm of the mistake which has been caused. To rebuke, curse or beat someone in front of others is totally wrong. It damages more than it corrects.

4. **Rightful Earning:** It is important that we earn our living through hard work and honesty. Money earned through improper means pollutes and corrupts everyone's mind and intellect. These faults then reveal themselves in the form of bad qualities in individuals and result in strives and ill-feeling among family members. Food earned through moral means provides ample mental and physical healthiness and nurture virtuous qualities in individuals.

Family life is like a sacred grove where the austerities of self-control, service and tolerance have to be performed.

— *Pt. Sriram Sharma Acharya*

---

22 — A Noble Art of Living

Human life is bestowed on us as an invaluable treasure of physical, intellectual, mental and spiritual powers. Most of us remain unaware of the capabilities and the mental powers hidden in our own self. Awakening and creative use of these resources leads to enormous success and unbelievable attainments in every dimension of life. This world is like a school of practical training, which offers enormous opportunities for refinement and development of talents and

Each day invest some time in realizing aim and purpose of your life.

potentials. Here, every human being is given the freedom to select the path of his life. But many fall prey to the vices of sensual pleasures and immoral activities driven by selfish motives and ambitions of power and money. He becomes victim of circumstances. Happy, healthy and blissful life can be possible if man adopts righteous attitude along with self-realization and self-reformation. If one introspects and resolves to improve behavior, talent and personality, he can achieve success, satisfaction and lead cheerful and glorious life.

Know Your True Value

A King went for hunting in a distance forest. He was trapped by wild animals and found helpless. He cried for help. Soon, a woodcutter came to rescue the King with fire and axes on his hands. Impressed with the woodcutter, the King gifted him a garden. The woodcutter was happy to get such a garden with big trees. But now the woodcutter thought, 'why should I take trouble of cutting the trees. Instead, I would burn them and do the business of charcoal.' Soon, he burnt the entire garden and earned some money by selling the charcoal. One day, when some wood could not be processed due to heavy rains, he took the wood pieces to sell in the market. The smell of wood pieces attracted big traders and he earned thousand times more than what he used to get from the charcoal. He was surprised to know that the wood pieces were actually sandalwood. Now, he was shocked to note his blunder and repented for burning sandalwood. We commit the same mistake every day in our life. We underestimate the importance of time in our life and waste precious moments in meeting selfish motives, which is far more precious than the sandalwood.

Traits for Wisest Act of Living

Self-retrospection: One can become a virtuous person if the time incurred in the appraisal of morality and immorality of others is used in self retrospection. Others' faults are easily visible, but own faults are visible only when our inner self is thoroughly introspected in specified manner. Traits like confidence and courage can be achieved by self inspiration only. Encouraging the efforts to grow the sentiments of self support feeds the life with strength to overcome distress.

Self-improvement: To get rid of the wild tendencies, to engender ascetic habits, and to remove own flaws, one has to succumb to the process of self improvement. One should go for thoughtful confrontation to come out of accustomed bad habits and to annihilate the activities inspiring them. As army clashes with enemy, likewise wild tendencies should be confronted with ascetic thoughts.

Self-dependence: Relying on self is such a mighty trait that it invokes courage, commitment and ability to carry out any work. So long you depend on others for resolution of problems, you are in deception. It is said that man makes his own destiny. If you want wealth, intellect, strength and wisdom then inculcate courage and skills. Start increasing your talent matching your ambitions. Every person has got ample autonomy to rise above the common stage and there is no reason you cannot succeed.

Self-confidence: Confidence stands for endurance and operating energy. Means are attempted to satisfy when anything is intensely desired and ultimately something comes as a solution. In this way, any job which seems difficult does not remain more than a normal fork for a determined person. Confidence generates courage, valiancy, energy, productivity, strength, and activates hidden source of power. A strong desire to achieve the target is a vital force which alone paves its ways.

> ### Significance of Human Life
>
> Suppose a father credits $1440 every day into son's bank account with a faith that his son would make best utilization of the money. After few years, he observes that his son has lost the entire amount in gambling. Do you believe that the father would provide the same facility to his son in the future? Probably not. In the similar way, God credits 1440 minutes every day in our life's account. Most of us are ignorant about aim and purpose of life. In rare cases, we help others without any selfish motive. Hence, a deeper introspection is needed to recognize the true importance of human life.

Our hopes should be like hair and nails. No matter how many times they get cut, but they never stop growing.

Win Over Your Weaknesses

○ **Arrogance:** Arrogance is an image of self-respect in the mirror of complacence, illusions and artificiality. Driven by superiority feeling, one tends to underestimate others by influence of intelligence, wealth, and powerful status. In this way, an arrogant fellow keeps increasing his enemies without any substantial reason. Ego overshadows all his good qualities and personality and cause major distraction from path of success.

Accepting your weaknesses is sign of real progress in life.

○ **Ignorance:** Ignorance is the root cause of most suffering. People often spend many years of their lives totally immersed in an illusionary, deceptive world. They lack right knowledge and rational approach toward issues in day-to-day life. To get rid of ignorance, one must expand knowledge and kill arrogance. Keep faith on your capabilities and be compassionate.

○ **Fallacious attractions:** As the earth has its gravitational force, the world has its own attractions. Most of us fail to overcome untoward thoughts and join the race of attaining momentary joy and satisfaction. The sheep blindly follow their rabble and fall in the ditch one after another. One must develop confidence to overcome these attractions and follow righteous path.

○ **Fear and anxiety:** The flow of life progresses like a swing, sometimes there are favorable circumstances and sometimes contrary. People often fall victim of fear, despair, depression in the face of a tragedy or adversities. You cannot know and judge your real potentials until there are testing moments. On introspection, you will find self-obsession, impatience, shortsightedness and unnecessary imaginations as root cause of your tensions. So, do not let the negative tendencies envelop the elixir of immense joy and happiness in your life.

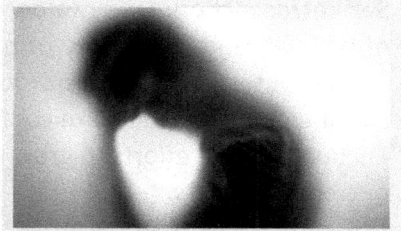

You hold the key to perfect life

Men are taught from childhood that they are weak and fragile. We are there where destiny has brought us. This kind of thinking reflects one's lack of faith on his own potentials. You should have faith in your soul. This will help you cultivate the seeds of courage, optimism and vivacity in your inner spirit. It is only you who could make yourself happy. When you think and attempt for inner content and happiness, it indeed rejuvenates your mind. Look at the lives of great personalities, the intrepid warriors, who won against all odds. You have all the capabilities to eliminate your poverty, your weakness and adversities; you only need to recognize this fact and change your attitude and routine accordingly. You are the creator of your own destiny.

Sustenance of Good Health: Wisest Act of Living

It is well known that healthy body and sound mind are necessary for progress in every walk of life. Various types of enjoyments and riches are available in this world but what is the use of them if there is no strength or ability to enjoy them? Nature has innately gifted all living creatures with vibrant health. Upon investigating the physiques of all the creatures, it appears that only humans suffer from different kind of illness and weaknesses. Even tiniest and weakest creatures roam around naked during winter and summer; but none gets affected by pneumonia or struck by heat stroke. It proves that the original strength of any person is good health. One must follow nature's way of living and stick to some rules for maintaining healthy lifestyle.

Healthy body and mind is capable of creating healthy thoughts.

(1) Select right food: Foods are the fuel of body engine. One must take food with plenty of fiber, such as whole-grain breads, cereals, and beans, and consume adequate fluid to clean toxins. Make a calorie chart for your body and select the food rich in vitamin, carbohydrate, and protein. Avoid consuming excess food. A balanced diet will develop immunity and keep the body fit.

(2) Physical activity: If a machine is kept idle for a long time, it catches rust and unable to work properly. The same rule applies to human body also. In order to retain flexibility of all muscles in the body, it is essential to engage in physical work or exercises. To revive respiratory and circulatory systems and boost immunity, one needs to avoid lethargy and indulge in appropriate physical activity.

(3) Management of daily routine: Regular and disciplined life saves a person from clutches of many diseases. Cleanliness, purity and sanctity produce beneficial effects on health. Rooms should be well ventilated to allow fresh air and sunlight. Over sleeping and late night work also affects our metabolic activities.

(4) Stress-free mind: A person who maintains calm, cheerful, happiness and full of hope always keeps himself healthy. Laughter is the best medicine for mind and body. One should always hope for brighter future. Sorrow, grief, distress, anxiety are top enemies for good health. A perturbed, worried and feeble mind casts its influence on the organs of the body.

As the blueprint of a tree is coded in its seed, the infinite potentials of progress are hidden in all human beings.

— *Pt. Sriram Sharma Acharya*

23   Refinement and Improvement of Talents

Amongst the many types of resources acquired by man, talent is unique. Wealth keeps changing with time, physical attraction remains till young age and even intimacy with anyone proves worthless sometime or other. Memory, intelligence, hard work too make a fast exit. Efforts made in augmentation of talents can be encashed for success in any field of human activity. Miracles of the materialist world are only because

Talents are not inherited; it is harnessed by firm determination and right attitude.

of the endeavors of talents. Talents do not descend down on a person from heaven. They are acquired with hard endeavour, persistent efforts, and firm determination. A valuable possession of merits is understood to be most precious treasure of human life. Undoubtedly you will be honoured if you try your best to develop your excellence. People give credit to virtues not individuals. One should always closely observe whenever virtuality and merits emerge in the inner self and should try to nurture that.

Misutilization of talents

Talent is sometimes misutilized for improper objectives. Here, talent must always be understood as an integrated development of idealistic intellect and emotions. Wealth, strength, and expertise are also being used for destructive purposes. In course of time such persons suffer from remorse, ignominy and punishment despite accumulation of wealth. Therefore, persons having farsighted prudence can only make an endeavor to develop positive attributes and engage in idealistic activities.

Do not waste your time in waiting for an opportunity. Create one right now.

Five Steps for Improvement of Talents

(1) Augmentation of capabilities: Each job requires specified skill set. Improvement in desired skills begins with self-esteem, dedication and regular practice. Rise in capabilities enhances confidence and provide encouragement to set higher goals.

(2) Planning and orderliness: Only those persons are considered worthy of shouldering big responsibilities who

Realizing your worth is first step in improvement of talents.

develops capacity to plan and organize their efforts, resources, thoughts and surrounding environment by providing them the right direction. Such persons are aware that for being progressive one has to change strategy according to circumstances and improve upon existing methodology.

(3) Positive attitude: Talented persons are always found radiating happiness. He maintains humility and respect for every human being. It becomes feasible only for those who are constantly inspired by seeing qualities in others and believe in self-reformation. With the result, others too look forward to them for alleviating their misery.

(4) Courage: No one is known to have inherited talents for performing significant tasks. Extraordinary talents develop only in those persons who develop unusual courage to undertake big challenges. Courage imparts capacity to upgrade character and simultaneously develop conviction, motivation and hard endeavor to achieve multifaceted success in all walks of life.

(5) Introspection: To become capable at mental plane, develop the habit of introspection because it helps promote one's abilities and hidden talents. Identify what is your special talent, your innate aptitude and set about to work on that.

Take up one idea. Make that one idea your life – think of it, dream of it, live on that idea. Let the brain muscles, nerves, every part of your body, be full of that idea, and just leave every other idea alone. You will achieve the goal soon.

— *Swami Vivekananda*

Principles of Talent Refinement

Human being is a storehouse of powers of limitless capacities. But in the absence of true effort, it is difficult to boost righteous traits and eliminating evil tendencies hindering improvement of talents and intellectual capabilities. Everyone must try to adopt some principles for happy, progressive and successful life.

(1) The first pre-requisite for refinement of talents is persistence struggle against habit of laziness, ignorance, despair, apprehension. Cleanliness of body, purity of mind, observance of civility and good conduct are necessary to develop true talent.

(2) Talented person does not sit waiting for other people's support; instead moves forward forcing them to join along in his endeavours. Overdependence on any person or resource and avoiding risks and responsibility reduces creative abilities.

(3) Talented people constantly review their actions and activities and adopt whatever changes they find necessary in them. They never have a fixating thinking.

(4) People often fail and earn ridicule because of their disorganized state of mind and quality of work. Those who can properly manage their time, efforts, resources, thoughts, and family relations, can alone be expected to bear higher or bigger responsibilities. By adopting the principle of simple living and high thinking, one could enhance noble qualities and serve others.

Story: King and the wood cutter

Once upon a time, a king hired a woodcutter with a contract of cutting 10 trees every day. On first day, the woodcutter cut 10 trees but on second day he cut only 8 trees. The king asked to exert more energy and time to meet the target. But despite hard work, the number of trees decreased on subsequent days. The king came to forest and asked the woodcutter the reason behind decrease in quantity. Probe revealed that the woodcutter missed sharpening of axes before cutting the trees. We often make the similar mistakes. We believe in hard work to perform a task but forget to sharpen our skills on daily basis. If we make a habit to improve quality along with dedication and hard work, we can win the race easily.

Do You Know?

- Albert Einstein did not read until he was seven and expelled from the school
- Abraham Lincoln lost his business twice, lost seven elections, underwent nervous breakdown but at last became highly successful President of the United States

Scientific Ways To Nurture Talent

○ **Autosuggestion:** One becomes, what one thinks. Autosuggestion is the method to use positive words and sentences repeatedly to change perception. The entire crux of mental transformation lies hidden in autosuggestion. Avoid using words, 'I can't do this,' instead use 'I will try'.

○ **Contemplation of great people:** Reading and analyzing qualities of great people who served country for larger interest of society helps in developing similar traits within us.

○ **Spirit for bright future:** When spirit emerges from within, it erupts like a spark of fire that rises and expands unhindered. It transforms one's life in a stormy way. This spirit of spring induces inspiring enthusiasm and enchanting, enlightening emotional thrust in every heart.

○ **Time management:** Manage your time by preparing time table. Fix your priorities a day before important works. Meet deadlines and strictly adhere to routine. Multitasking habit can save lots of precious time.

Traits for Augmentation of Talent

Human being is a storehouse of powers of limitless capacities. But in the absence of true effort, it is difficult to boost righteous traits and eliminating evil tendencies hindering improvement of talents and intellectual capabilities. Talents are made to grow from within. However, it requires removal of those obstacles which offer resistance to one attempting to achieve excellence. A student of self-development should stick to following rules to eliminate weaknesses and boost inner strength:

(a) **Crow Effort:** Having seen an eatable lying on land, a crow hurriedly reaches there even flying high in the sky and achieves its target. Likewise, one should also have a strong desire to gain knowledge and proceed ahead to achieve high target in life.

(b) **Heron Concentration:** A heron very attentively stands on one leg on the banks of a pond or river. Immediately on becoming aware of a fish, it captures it and again rolls back in earlier posture. A learner should also be attentive and proceed consistently on the path of progress while gaining the knowledge of their subject.

(c) **Dog Sleep:** As a sleeping dog awakens even with hissing of sound near it, like that a learner should always remain alert and conscious to achieve the goal of life. He should have a sincere sleep.

(d) **Low Diet:** One who wants to attain above mentioned state should consume plain, sanctimonious and low quantity of food. A person who takes excess quantity of food invites laziness as his life-force is consumed in digestion, sleep and sluggishness. He should always adhering to instructions of healthiness.

24   Golden Rules of Self-Development

A human being is a unique entity amongst the living species of the world capable of performing wonders. There are many instances of men achieving seemingly impossible tasks by sheer power of will. Whoever has made progress in any field or achieved a status in society has to develop prudence for self-evolution and courage to confront with difficulties, resolve problems and circumvent the obstacles in one way or the other. No one is ever born talented. Nor is talent obtained as a gift or lucky coincidence. It is a

If man could realize importance of human life, he can't spoil single moment.

resource acquired through one's own endeavor. In order to make talents efficacious, one needs restructuring of the continuous process for improvement of the inner-self along with remodeling of one's style of living. One who makes a perseverant effort to develop mental faculties and developing them progressively shoulders and fulfills greater responsibilities, acquires an efficacious organizational skill, by virtue of which wherever he goes, he is bound to be crowned with success.

Mind Your Thought

Negative thinking is regarded as disorder of the subtle body, which upsets psychology and brain functions. Research in endocrinology and neurology indicates negative thoughts disrupt flow of bioelectricity across the neurons. This causes imbalance in hormonal secretion and leads to psychosomatic abnormalities. On contrary, refined thought, altruistic ideology and generous attitude improve physical and mental health. Dr. Viktor Frankl devised a kind of psychotherapy called Logotherapy to treat patients with mental imbalances. Dr. Frankl laid emphasis on making the patient realize the importance and purpose of life. In Logotherapy, the doctor tries to recognize factors triggering hatred, fear, and dejection in the patient's mind. Accordingly, the patient is offered counseling and moral support to bring back light of hope in his life. In this way, disorders like depression, anxiety, Obsessive-compulsive disorder, and Schizophrenia are treated effectively.

Powers You Must Possess

○ **The Power of Vision:** A fast pace horse running in wrong direction will never reach its destination. It is important to understand that the power of vision depends on your thought process, awareness about field, and capability to visualize the future. Empowering your thought involves positive attitude, meeting with learned people, watching relevant documentaries, reading good books and watching news regularly develop your vision.

○ **The Power of 'Now':** People make plans but they never execute them. They keep thinking and waiting for the 'right' moment to kick off their plans. The best way to make your dreams come true is to wake up and act. It is true that planning is significant to achieve high big targets. Break down the big target into smaller tasks and start implementing one by one. If you keep waiting for good time, you may face tougher circumstance next day. So, 'Now' is the best time to execute your planning.

○ **The Power of Positivity:** Successful people posses a positive mindset. Remember that being positive will give you the freedom to look forward instead of looking backward. Positive people convert risks into opportunities. They have the sense of responsibility and gratitude. They believe in developing skills rather to depend on luck. To develop this quality, try staying away from negative-minded people, read wisdom quotes and accept tough challenges.

Everyone dreams for success, few hold confidence to convert them in reality.

○ **The Power of Analytics:** One must develop the power to evaluate present condition or a problem to secure future. It includes breaking the bigger problems into smaller tasks, considering the issue from wider and multiple angles, differentiating between urgent and important tasks and eventually working on things which matter the most. There is no problem without a solution. You must develop creative ideas and approach for effective resolution of issues.

During a game of chess one is required to keep an eye on all the boxes. The player concentrating on only immediate moves disregarding the subsequent and the consequent moves, is easily checkmated. Each assignment of our life is like a game of chess. One is required to keep an eye on each related aspect. The conceptual capacity is to be enlarged to an extent wherein each possible change in situation is anticipated in detail. Similarly, big meetings, public celebrations, and festivals necessitate multi-faceted arrangements. Only those who have the capacity to conceptualize all aspect of a project are acclaimed for success.

Traits for Self-Improvement

Learning Skills: To achieve high objectives, the distracted mental energy should be channelized. This is achieved by constant practice of learning. Learning is a continuous process that commences at birth and continues until death. Strong learning skills and positive work habits are often an indicator of future success. Learning is an internal activity and therefore, it is not something that can be directly observed in others. For effective learning process one needs to nurture curiosity and deep interest in the subject. Curiosity "to know" will naturally cause a person to ask questions and enhance learning capability.

Organizational Skill: For success in any field of human endeavor, the significance of resources can hardly be underrated. However, it must be understood that best utilization of available resources in the existing circumstances is a great art. With the organization of body and mind, one attains the initial half of success. A man needs to develop organizational skill along with expertise, extra diligence, and perseverance to achieve target. It is the efficiency of planning and good organization of resources, which enables man to be happy and successful.

Concentration Power: Sunlight scatters everywhere but if allowed to pass through a convex lens, it can ignite fire. Human mind works in similar pattern. Mind is endowed with tremendous strength. The more concentrated it is, the more power is brought to bear on one point. One who has good concentration can recollect and remember information better and faster. Artisans like blacksmith, barbers, carpenters, and goldsmith, pilots, shooters, electricians and surgeons need high concentration power to successfully accomplish their work. In lack of concentration, they can either injure themselves or spoil materials. Concentrated mind delivers high quality of work and saves precious time.

Spiritual Insight: Spirituality is not an abstract philosophical subject for elevated soul. It concerns every facet of human life and should be adopted in every expression of our being. Spiritual books provide the indispensible motivation to continually recreate and mould our lives. The presence of good thoughts suppresses the bad. Not only literature, but a deep conviction in a Higher Being deters us from straying onto the wrong path. Therefore, every single person must do daily prayer before going to sleep.

What is real success?

Everyone has its own yardstick for measuring his success. In the eyes of the world, success is defined by "what a person has", but in reality it is measured by "what a person is". People believe that those who are successful are happy. But a deeper observation will find it to be not true. New desires take shape in our body every day. Once that desire is fulfilled, again a new sense of dissatisfaction overtakes us. It means that we are becoming more successful but our sense of satisfaction is becoming lesser. Success makes life meaningful, only when it will give a feeling of contentment. One should set goals based on his unique traits, strengths, and abilities to achieve real success and satisfaction.

Tips for Self-Empowerment

○ Believe that you are the most important person in this world. You are not another person in crowed. Understand that if you really try, you can accomplish anything you would like to do.

○ Spend some time in analyzing your aim and purpose in life. Introspect your habits, strengths and weaknesses, vision, behavior and try to improve upon each element every day.

○ Live each day as if it's your last. Seize every moment and try to make best use of each opportunity with maximum potential.

○ Know what you are capable of. Become the master of your domain by developing interest and regular practice.

○ Love yourself and give love to everyone. Love without expecting anything in return.

The power of your creative imagination

The mind keeps flying on the wings of imaginations. Most of the imaginations remain in the state of never-to-be-materialized dreams and keep tantalizing the inner consciousness time and again. In the experience of the select few, imagination is the divine potency of human consciousness. By imaginations, new creative energies sprout forth, the arts are created, the foundation of research is laid and innovations are made. The first step on the path of all achievements is taken on the basis of imagination power. The meeting of imagination with intellect opens new vistas of scientific and technological advancement. When the waves of imaginations arising in the mind are chiseled by the intellect and synthesized, and then channeled into a focused direction, imagination takes the right shape. It forms the basis of self-development and one may reap following benefits by using imagination power:

1. Development of creative and analytical skills in life through imaginations.

2. Finding solutions of problems of day-to-day life and developing insight into the secrets of life.

3. Make yourself bold and strong by forceful imaginations. The inner determination gives strength to remain unruffled in the face of crisis.

4. Imaginations make you visualize about virtuous qualities lacking in the personality. It also develops vision to improve upon habits, attitude and thought process.

He alone lives a worthwhile life, who has a cool head, warm blood, a loving heart, and zest for life.
　　　　　　　　　　　　　　　　　　　　　　　　—*Pt. Sriram Sharma Acharya*

25 | Mental Health Management

The melodious music of life is played on the instrument of sound mental health. A self-disciplined and illuminated mind is treasure trove of unlimited human powers in world. Mental health includes emotional, psychological, and social well-being of a person. Any kind of progress – temporal or spiritual is conditional on good mental health. Money, fame, power knowledge, all depends on vibrant mental and physical health of the individual. But in spite of common knowledge,

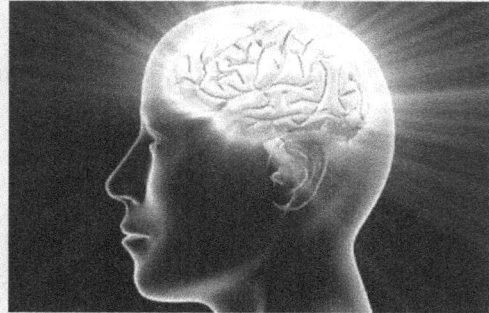
An illuminated mind inspires the path of development and leads to all-round success.

most of the people are negligent about their health as they lack a holistic vision of life. The state and activities of the mind affect the body and those of the latter influence the mind in return. One's inner desires, convictions, thoughts are constantly inscribed in the inner core of the mind and influence future course of life. The world around us is nothing but a shadow or a reflection of our mind. Therefore, managing mental health is significant in keeping our thoughts, emotions and objective on track.

Mental Health Problems

Mental health affects how we think, feel and act as we cope with life. It also helps determine how we handle stress, relate to others, and make choices. However, many things that happen in your life can disrupt emotional health and lead to strong feelings of sadness, stress or anxiety. It includes accident or death of loved one, exam fever, financial or health issues, losing job etc. If mind is depressed, the body will also become inactive. The agile mind is the most dreaded enemy of the individual self. Now-a-days, mental health problems are rising fast as people find it difficult to manage day-to-day stress and anxiety. The common psychiatric disorders due to adoption of modern lifestyle include Depression, Anxiety Disorders, Schizophrenia, Bipolar Disorder (Manic-Depressive Illness), and even suicide. Therefore, one should analyze and adopt efficient ways to tackle mental health risks.

How to Manage Mental Imbalances

Managing Thoughts and Behaviour: The quality of our mental inscriptions and hence the nature of our mind depends upon what kind of thoughts dominate our mind. You must ponder over this fact that your mental evolution is in your hands. Once you realize the hidden power of your thoughts and pay attention to their righteous orientation, many of your problems would be solved in no time. Short-temperedness enhances the tendencies of anger and mental imbalance. Worries, gloom, despair, and similar kinds of negative instincts weaken your mind further. Positive,

The agile mind is the most dreaded and nearest enemy of the individual self.

optimistic and reasoned thinking educes new joy and energy in your mind and motivates for constructive actions. Concentration upon a focused objective augments corresponding skills and potentials. Good or bad, beauty or ugliness, superiority or inferiority are all creations of our own thoughts. Now it is the right time we improve ourselves right from the root of our thinking rather than attributing our failures to – ill omen or lack of resources or support.

Managing Emotions: Anxiety, fear, despair, fury, cowardice, depression etc are common reactions of most people in the face of a tragedy or adversities. Another extreme of uncontrolled minds is expressed as an outburst of ego, audacity, jealousy, insecurity, craze for luxurious life and so on. Stout lockers are designed and used for keeping safe the cash, jewelry, and other valuables. It will be absurd if some filth is stored in it. Our mind is also like a locker and one needs to acquire purity of mind to keep quality thoughts in it. Wearing clean cloths and being orderly and tidy gives a feeling of alacrity, similarly, virtuous thoughts and deeds also magnify and inspire divine feelings and illuminate inner self.

Managing Stress: Stress is a state of mental or emotional strain due to adverse situations in our lives. The principal cause of stress is adoption of artificial and unhealthy life-style, high expectations and over-dependence on resources. Stress not only causes mental imbalance but the primary cause of many avoidable health problems. Wrong attitude and pessimistic thoughts cause emotional stress, which ultimately lead to psychosomatic illness and change our behaviour pattern. If you introspect, you will discover that it is your expectations to others, self-obsession, and impatience as the main cause of stress. Keep your thought process healthy and broad. Laughter is the best natural medicine to reduce stress. Learn and practice relaxation techniques and perform Yoga, Meditation, and Prayer regularly to rejuvenate mind and body.

129

Nutrition and Mental Health

Purity of food helps in purifying the inner self and hence the mind and intellect. Intrinsic qualities of food, timing of food taken as well as mood during eating process not only affects physical health but also mental state. The same food would have healthier effects if eaten in happy mood, whereas mental excitement, disturbance would make it harmful or less suitable for our health. If there is any sentiment of jealousy, fear, anger, greed, lust, gloom, sorrow, hatred, etc, then the food consumed cannot be digested properly and causes acidity, constipation etc. Deep fried food, varieties of spices and arbitrary combination of foods of non-compatible natural qualities are also harmful to our mental and physical health. The use of pre-cooked food-ingredients and the so called "fast foods" have very adverse effects on our body system. Always take fresh food to make your mind 'fresh' and active. To boost mental power, desist from toxic substances such as tobacco, alcoholic drinks, and betel leaves. Stimulants such as caffeine, tobacco, and nicotine stimulate release of stress hormone and causes Adrenal Fatigue. Vegetarian food items are best for enhancing mental strength.

How to Enhance Memory Power

Sharp memory is regarded as a sign of brilliance and intellectual talents, which are key factors of successful life. Adept learning and refinement of talents also requires sound and trenchant memory. For instance, many students fail in examinations due to lack of memory power despite hard work. Healthy and active senses are prime means of our development. But it must not be forgotten that their motivator is our mind. To make best use of mind in improving memory power and self-development one should follow some guidelines:

1. **Develop Interest:** The desire to learn is prerequisite to raise intellectual capabilities and memory. It imparts motivation and opens up the progressive path of knowledge acquisition. Knowledge is pervaded everywhere in the cosmos. One needs to develop earnest desire and alertness of mind to attract the resources of the Universe. If we are half asleep, bored or inattentive while listening to a lecture, we cannot remember any part of it.

2. **Avoid Stress:** The elements of brain are sensitive to mental excitations and negative feelings. Over-ambitiousness and worries weaken mental stability. Aspirants of healthy mind and sharp memory should protect themselves from mental malice, anxiety, jealousy, and other factors affecting our thought process. Chronic stress destroys brain cells and damages the hippocampus, the region of the brain involved in the formation of new memories and the retrieval of old ones.

3. **Master a New Skill:** Learning new skills time-to-time helps in development of cognitive abilities. With practice and experience new connection between neurons are made and it improves intelligence. Try to involve more sense organs in learning process. Never get satisfied with what you have learnt. Be innovative.

Mind-Boosting Nutrients

A balanced mood and feelings of wellbeing can be protected by ensuring that our diet provides adequate amounts of complex carbohydrates, essential fats, amino acids, vitamins and minerals and water. The major ingredients of food most suitable for making the mind healthy and fit are:

Folate (Folic Acid, Vitamin B9): Increased intake of folate is associated with a lower risk of depression. Spinach, turnip, mustard greens, fruits, nuts, beans are high in folic acid.

Omega-3 Fatty Acids: Flaxseeds, walnuts, soybeans, navy beans are rich sources of omega-3 fatty acids. One-quarter cup of flaxseeds contains about 6.3 grams of omega-3 fatty acids.

Whole Grains: The primary source of energy for the brain is glucose, which comes from carbohydrates. Simple carbohydrates exacerbate low mood by creating spikes in blood sugar and have been shown to have effects on the brain similar to drugs of abuse. By contrast, complex carbohydrates release glucose slowly, helping us feel full longer and providing a steady source of fuel for the brain and body. Healthy sources of complex carbohydrates include whole-wheat products, bulgur, oats, wild rice, barley, beans and soy.

Protein: The food we eat is broken down into substances that are used to make neurotransmitters and other chemicals that allow different parts of the nervous system to communicate effectively with each other and the rest of the body. Next to carbohydrates, protein is the most abundant substance in the body. The amino acid tryptophan, a building block of protein, influences mood by producing the neurotransmitter serotonin. Milk, eggs, yogurt, soya, fish and sea food, beans, lentils, and green peas are rich protein sources.

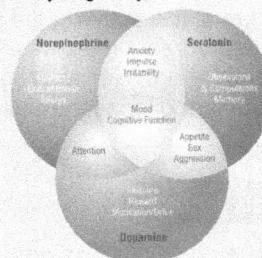

Are your neurotransmitters getting the specific amino acids and associated neuro-nutrients they need to give you happy, calm and focused thoughts every single day?

Mind Your Stress

When we are exposed to stress, our body releases the stress hormones cortisol and adrenaline to alleviate the stress level. In this process, the pulse rate and blood pressure increase as part of body's defence mechanism. If we are frequently exposed to stress conditions, the level of stress hormones rises, which can lower body's immune system and affect proper functioning of brain. It has been found that high level of stress hormones leads to loss of brain cells and impairs brain function. It also causes the body and brain to age more quickly.

Quick Fact

Positive thoughts release neuropeptides that help fight stress and potentially more-serious illnesses.

Tricks to Improve Brain-Health

○ Be regular in physical exercise and engage in activities to develop mental skills

○ Keep stress in check, avoid anxiety in all day-to-day matters

○ Take complex carbohydrates such as whole-wheat bread, brown rice, oatmeal, and whole beans

○ Keep confidence level high and do not underestimate your abilities

○ Prohibit yourself from smoking, tobacco, alcohol and other narcotics

○ Laughter is the best tonic for brain. It increases oxygen supply to brain, relaxes muscles, decreases stress and lowers blood pressure

How Exercise Boosts Mind Power

Physical and mental exercises are believed to boost secretion of chemical called Brain-Derived Neurotrophic Factor (BDNF), which encourages formation of new neurons in brain. BDNF is also protective to neurons in anxiety and stress conditions. BDNF improves learning and memory power by strengthening communication between neurons. In the brain, it is active in the hippocampus, cerebral cortex, and basal forebrain—areas vital to learning, memory, and higher thinking. Hence, regular exercises are linked to development of concentration and memory.

Do You Know?

The human brain has an astonishing ability to adapt and change—even into old age. This ability is known as neuroplasticity. When stimulated, the human brain will generate new neurons through this process. A new brain connection is made between two or more brain cells each time you have a new thought or memory. You can harness the natural power of neuroplasticity to increase your cognitive abilities and improve your memory.

The powers of the mind are like the rays of the sun. When they are concentrated, they illumine.

— *Swami Vivekananda*

26 Proceed in Righteous Path

Life's True Ambition

The family of the problems created by insatiable desires is infinite. Take money for example. It is required for the smooth maintenance of our and our family's living. A man must maintain one's life according to one's income and be satisfied with it. He must use his remaining energy for own salvation and social welfare. But, who, in reality, does this? Accumulating wealth and then blowing it up is so pleasing to them that they are always eager for acting that way.

If you want to live happy life, tie it to a goal, not to people or things.

Money promotes happiness only when it is at the command of people with noble thoughts and concern for humanity. If basic necessities of life are considered, enough time is available for the salvation of a person whose ambition is limited to feed and clothe his family suitable. The tornado of ambitions and lusts sweeps away man's virtuous strength. If one can free oneself from these poisonous influences, then sufficient time is available in which to think and do salvation. Utilise this body in the shape of his image for doing something immortal. It is a misconception to believe that once there is enough wealth, every-one would be happy.

Talk to yourself at least once a day...otherwise, you may miss a meeting with an excellent person!

—*Swami Vivekananda*

Fight Your Ego

The greatest obstacle in man's spiritual upliftment is his egoistic thinking. Conflicts, troubles wars and word-wars have been spending their terror in this world because of such egoistic feelings as, "I am the monarch of all I survey", "my thoughts are superior to other's thoughts", I am the most beautiful", "I am wealthy", I am knowledgeable" etc. Is the arrogance really justifiable? There are so many people more beautiful, more capable and with greater powers than yours. Then what is your ego going to achieve?

The pride or arrogance of prosperity, beauty, personality, or knowledge is that vice which keeps us away from the real knowledge of life. Man must always keep before him the transitoriness, the impermanence of everything and save himself from the bad influence of the ego. Spiritual progress and self-realisation are achieved only by such people as can subordinate their base instincts to higher emotions.

Develop Foresightedness

It is unwise desire for quick profit without caring to think about the future, man starts doing bad deeds. One must seriously think that if death were to strike us right now, how will our presently troubling problems, ambitions and the worries be solved?

Life has been described as a mere bubble of water, and this is not untrue. We see death striking youngsters in the prime of their lives and see their funerals passing by. We see children like delicate flowers wilting away. Is it certain that we will get a chance to live a hundred years when we see the funerals of young men and delicate children passing by? The moot thought is that when death strikes, you will not be there to solve any of the problems. Therefore, a man should look into the future, think in advance about the possible result of today's work and then act with discretion.

Walk Alone, Never Depend on Anybody

Great men go on their paths because they walk alone. Their inspiration comes from within. They alone spur their happiness and remove their sadness and they are helped along only by their own ideas. Loneliness is undeniable truth of life. Everybody has to make their own path of progress. What you believe to be loneliness is actually a kind of solitude, given to you to develop your own inner strength. When you are left alone, you can better realize your inner strength and weaknesses. Putting your life in another person's hand is like setting sail without knowing where you are going. The day you develop faith in the strength of your own hands, feet and heart, your soul will tell you to go forth alone.

Who is Spiritual?

If we want to get pleasure out of everything surrounding us, it is possible once we start loving everyone around us. If we can get over our narrow selfishness, the whole world would belong to us and everything that makes some one happy would be a source of happiness to us. Then, there will be infinite sources dishing out happiness to us all the time. This is the crux of good citizenship and true morality. It is very important that human relations become cordial for once that happen, mutual understanding and cooperation would invariably follow. The

Real purpose of spirituality is to motivate mankind to achieve altruism.

path to perpetual peace has to be laid with human virtues. This is the main objective of spirituality.

"Who is the smallest one in this world?"A devotee asked this question to Lord Buddha. He replied, "One who thinks of himself and thinks only his self-interest as most important."In these few words, Buddha drew the outlines of practical spiritualism. Why should we not feel all the people of this earth as our family? Why should we feel the lack of friends, sons and near ones? What is seen outside is merely the reflection of what is within. Spiritualism is nothing but seeking and identifying this treasure, developing it and spreading love all around us.

How to Make Your Life an Offering

To make your life offering, make sure that you comply with the following,

- See every person as worthy of kindness
- Utilize your time with honesty and discipline
- Work for the welfare of needy people
- Constantly keep God in your thoughts
- Stay focused on your duties
- Maintain your mental equilibrium and manage stress effectively
- Make spiritual books your best friend and consult them whenever you need guidance

Gladly Accept Life's Challenges

To most of us the hardships, adversities and challenges of life seem to be intractable like gigantic mountains, dreadful like wild giants, but this is all subject to how we take them. Its ironical that many people prefer suffering hardship and scarcity instead of doing hard work, because they somehow regard physical labor as something below their prestige. These insane convictions are harmful not only to the individuals but also to the society as a whole. The secret of success of the societies and nations seen as developed or progressing is that they respect and adopt hard labor – be that physical or mental – in all walks of life.

Do not treat yourself as feeble, incapable or helpless. Renounce the weaker thoughts like, 'how can I proceed without amenities?' Always remember that source of strength is not in amenities but lies in determination. Just change your attitude and you will find hope, courage and enthusiasm in all circumstances. Don't lose your morale that you failed in your repeated attempts. There are many other venues. Look at them. You just have to try your level best in transacting your duties. Every sincere effort is a step towards the goal; if not today, tomorrow you will succeed.

Astrology and Hard Work

A King was firm believer of Astrology. He did all his work on specific time and always kept one astrologer as his aid. One day they were going somewhere. They saw one farmer going to his fields with plough and ox. Astrologer asked him, "Today the celestial condition is not suitable in this direction. Go back; otherwise be ready to bear the losses. Farmer replied, "It's my routine to go to fields. Celestial conditions can do no harm to me. I just work hard every day and earn bread irrespective of positions of planets." Astrologer and King were ashamed and admitted the superior prowess of farmer.

The only source of knowledge is Experience.   — *Albert Einstein*

Youth period is the finest period in human life. Full of vigor and enthusiasm, youths have the unequalled zeal, which could even confront the mountains. Their physical and mental capabilities get expressed in various ways and could turn even the most impossible task into a reality. They naturally posses the qualities required to carry on the complete transformation of their society. There are numerous virtuous youths in our nation. The only requirement is to protect them from being spoiled. Also, youths, on

Not age but enthusiasm is measure of youthfulness.

their part, should try to come out clean, unaffected to their defiled surroundings. If they understand the ill effects of wickedness at the right time and stop craving for materialistic pleasures, then no one could drive them on the wrong path. A tree would develop according to the quality of its seed. It would blossom and bear fruits according to the variety of the plantlet. Similarly, the foremost responsibility of the evil plight of the youth rests upon their parents and relatives. If they are themselves indulged in profanity, then how could they give good knowledge and values to their children?

Who is a Real Youth?

Youthfulness does not depend upon our small age but upon our ability to develop and progress. Development means to augment our latent energies and potentials. Progress means to constantly endeavor to increase our caliber. Senility does not imply an increase in age, but it is a synonymous to the lack of ability to develop and progress. A person who could make himself ingenuous, courageous, tolerant and honest would be eligible to serve his country and would be considered an eminent personality. Today's youth should invest some time and energy in self development and social reforms. Altruism and love for idealism is the first step for re-building social structure.

Root Cause of Social Degradation

Today, the opportunists, wicked and power hungry people could be seen everywhere, whether it is the field of social service, spirituality or politics. The education and health sectors, where the highest ideals of service were followed once, have now turned into the centers of professionalism and competition. Black marketing,

Stress Levels by Age

trickery, adulteration and tax evasion have become the basic rules of succeeding in business. The virtues of sacrifice, modesty, courteousness, benevolence, honesty and diligence are mocked at everywhere. From common citizen to the leaders dominating the corridors of power, almost everyone has become habitual to immorality and misconduct.

If we try to find out the reason behind this social degradation, we will find that it is wealth, which is the root cause of all these problems. It has become the most dominating factor in the world. People spend most of their time in thinking about strategies to maximize their earnings. For this, they don't even hesitate from employing nasty means like immorality, misconduct and corruption. This money, which is earned through faulty means, is the reason why the society is following worthless materialism and indulging excessively in pleasures. Though man understands this, yet he is crazy for wealth.

Moral Values vs Modernisation

In the previous times, while determining their role models, the youths had the support of their parents and the society. But today, no one wants to read and discuss about the ideal books like the Vedas, Upanishads, Quran and Bible. Even talking about them is considered a symbol of backwardness. People lack interest in the ideal and inspirational literature. While, the vulgar and down market text is flooding the markets, the tradition of reading sophisticated compositions is fast disappearing. Youth are confused as they don't know what to read and how to read? It is the outcome of neglecting our divine culture that today, while choosing his role model, a youth relies on the television and the films, instead of looking around for some ethical, valiant and eminent personality. There he gets nothing except violence, vulgarity, fashion and self-indulgence. So, he forms the conception that to be progressive means to follow these evils. This is the reason that we see the height of indiscipline and immorality all around us.

Challenges Before Today's Youth

Health Risks

Poor nutritional practices, cardiovascular diseases, obesity, anaemia, eating disorders, and conditions associated with affluence add to the burdens on today's youth. There are data available on the sexual activity of adolescents and unmarried young people from most parts of the world. According to UN report, young women aged 15-19 years give birth to approximately 17-million of

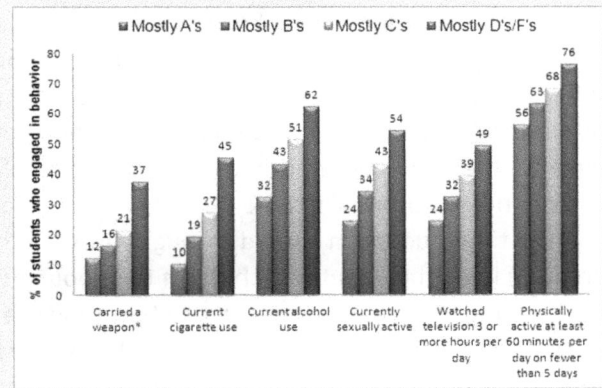

the 131-million children born every year. Anxiety and depression, stress and post-traumatic stress disorders combine with suicide, self-inflicted injury or other forms of violence (including homicide and the effects of self-administered abortion) to present one of the most disturbing faces of youth health. The influence exercised by cigarette manufacturers on the health behaviour of young people is disturbing. The use of tobacco is a major public health concern, yet because of clever advertising and misinformation in the media, young people fail to perceive themselves as being at high risk. Moreover, 5 million young people around the world are living with HIV. And with 41 percent of new HIV infections occurring among young people, that means every 30 seconds, another young person becomes HIV-positive.

Are You Getting True Education?

The youths of today are born amidst this defiled atmosphere and as they grow up, they have to face these painful and disturbing circumstances. They don't get the correct guidance from the immoral society. Moreover, the aimless education system confuses them further. To the youths of today, education is only a means to earn money. However, the actual utility of education lies in augmenting our knowledge and developing our talents and potentials so that we could benefit ourselves as well as the society. But today, education is being commercialized. People want to become doctors and engineers only because these professionals offer opportunities to earn lavishly. What is the use of such an education? One who aspires to get educated for the sake of the society deserves adoration. The aim should be determined after great deliberation. Many impediments would block our way, our opponents would create all sorts of problems, but if our determination is firm, all the bewilderments would vanish gradually.

Power of Youth

Youth sentiments have been the driving force behind all the major changes which have taken place and all the social, economic, religious and political revolutions which have occurred worldwide. When a handful of intellectual youths realized the need of the time and gave up their self centered interests and lustful life, then hundreds of monks came up and within a short span of time Buddhism spread throughout Asia. The credit of initiating about two-thirds of the population of the world to Christianity within two thousand years goes to only a few rational disciples of Jesus Christ. When Karl Marx died, only five to ten persons went to cremate him. But, when the intelligentsia realized the significance of his theories, then a big part of the world turned to communism.

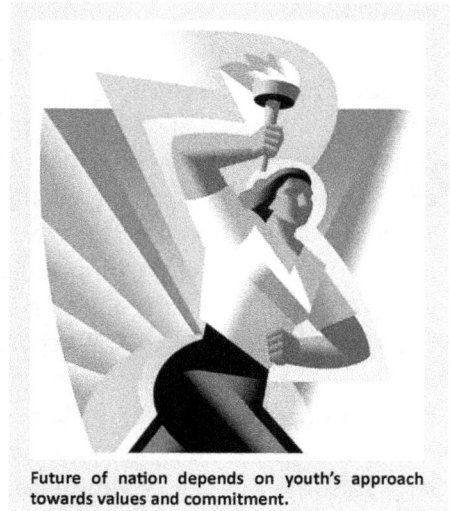

Future of nation depends on youth's approach towards values and commitment.

The chronicle of success written by Soviet Russia, an erstwhile world superpower, elaborates the undisputed role of youths in nation building. Whatever may be the present condition of partitioned Russia, but the unprecedented progress it witnessed between the four decades of 1920 to 1960 further exemplifies the potential of the youths. Over three-forth of its population was illiterate and poor in the beginning of the twentieth century. It lagged behind in the field of science and technology. The wave of revolution which appeared suddenly was the outcome of the organized youth revolution. Behind it was the glorious chapter of immense hard work, sacrifice and efforts of the youths.

Quick Fact

- Over 90% of smokers begin smoking before the age 19.
- 88% of young men and 74% of young women in custody had been excluded from school at some point.
- In the last decade in US, 284 kids were murdered due to school violence – these were shootings, stabbings, fighting and suicides.

Securing Future Generation

Today's greatest need is to arouse and rear wisdom in human beings. The virtues of nobility, compassion and kindness should be inculcated and encouraged to bloom. The moulding of men into good human beings is of far greater importance than establishing nuclear reactors. If we could build up an army of ideal social workers, the whole environment will gradually be transformed. If these committed men stand up and resolve to bring about revolutionary changes, the irrational customs, evil traditions, narrow-mindedness and crass selfishness will be washed out of the social system. The responsibility to lead the nation in the right direction has to shift from the political leadership to the elites, intelligentsia, religious teachers and nation builders who will not only deliver sermons, but will also concretely manifest the high ideas, and values of religion in their lifestyles. The time is not far off when religion will lead politics. Once these religious teachers are able to influence and inspire the public minds, they will guide politics on righteous lines.

Intellectuals' Role in Social Transformation

It is only the intellectual and sensitive youths, who could successfully eliminate the frustration of the society and infuse a new life into it. It is not possible to bring any revolutionary change without involving them. The second and a small group is that which can be called the elites, whose thoughts and feelings extend beyond the animal desires and vested interests to the higher realms of religion, society and culture. Elites are those who are moved by the prevailing pains, problems and evil tendencies plaguing the society and come forward to contribute their elimination. It is the need of the time that they endeavor enthusiastically to develop the society, converge all their scattered energies and try to solve the various problems of the society. Our progress is incorporated in the progress of our nation. Based on this broad-minded perspective, the youth power could manifest itself as the national power and take the nation on the path of prosperity and progress.

Those who have achieved harmony in their thoughts, words, and actions attain true awakening.

–*Pt. Sriram Sharma Acharya*

28   Yoga for Long and Healthy Life

Yoga is a mind-body practice that encompasses body movement, breathing techniques and relaxation to improve health. The philosophy and practice of Yoga date back to ancient times, originating perhaps as early as 5,000 to 8,000 years ago. Yoga helps in cleansing of the dirt and toxins deposited in various form and energises all components of the body. The defense and repair mechanism of the body are also strengthened by specific yoga poses. Yoga combines rigorous physical training with meditation practices, breathing, and sound/mantra techniques that lead to a mastery of the body, mind, and consciousness.

Initial Posture: Sit in a relaxed posture with erect spinal cord, neck and head straight and legs outstretched. Place the palms of the hand on the floor almost behind the buttocks; the elbows should be straight. Lean backwards taking support of the arms (Figure 1).

For Toes: Pay attention on your toes. Slowly move the toes of the both the feet backward and forward. The ankles should be kept naturally relaxed and stationary. Only the toes should move. Be attentive of your breaths. Inhale while the toes move backward and exhale as they move forward (Figure 2). Repeat it 5 to 10 times. Now, come back to initial posture.

For Ankles: Be seated in the 'initial posture' described in Figure 1. Slowly move the feet backward and forward by bending only near the ankles. Legs should remain outstretched and the knees should not bend. Heels should also remain stationary and touching the floor (Figure 3). Inhale during backward movement and exhale during forward. Repeat it 5 to 10 times.

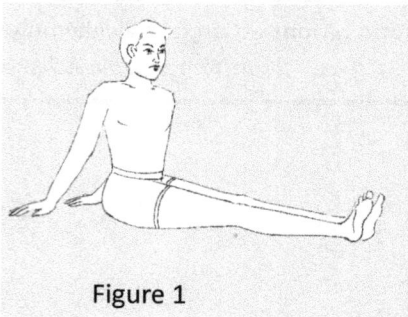

Figure 1

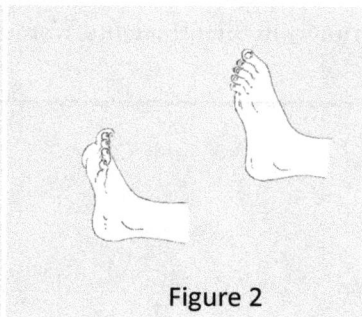

Figure 2

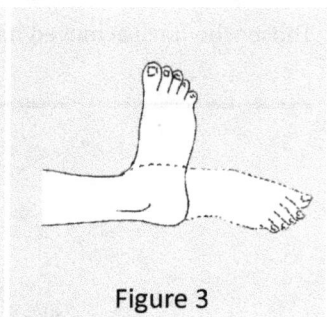

Figure 3

For Wrists: Straighten the arms in front at shoulder level. Close the fists with thumbs inside. Rotate the wrists clockwise for 10 times then anticlockwise (Figure 4).

For Elbows: Remain in sitting posture. Straighten the arms in front at shoulder level. Keep the palms open and facing up. Bend the arms at the elbows and touch the fingers to the shoulders without moving your body. Again straighten the arms (Figure 5). Repeat bending and straightening for 5 to 7 times.

For Shoulders: Keep the arms straight sideways at shoulder level. Throughout this exercise keep your head, neck and back straight. Bend the arms at elbows and touch the fingers to the shoulders. Now, rotate the bent arms first clockwise for 5-7 times and then anticlockwise (Figure 6). Return back to normal position after few seconds.

For Neck: Sit in straight posture. Slowly bend the head forward to make the chin touch as much near the lower edge of the neck as possible (Figure 7). Now, move the head backward as much as you can without straining. Bring the head back in normal position. Repeat 3 to 5 times. Now, slowly move the head to the right and bend it to attempt to make the right ear touch the right shoulder without lifting the shoulder. Bring the head back in normal position. Similarly, turn the head towards left and then bring it back to normal position. Repeat the same steps for 3-4 times.

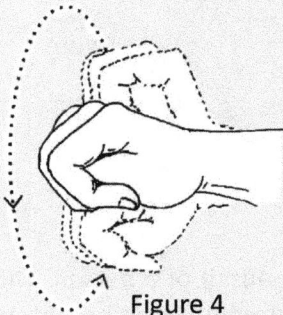
Figure 4

Figure 5

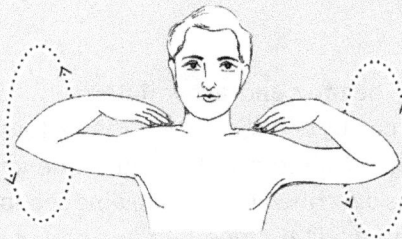
Figure 6

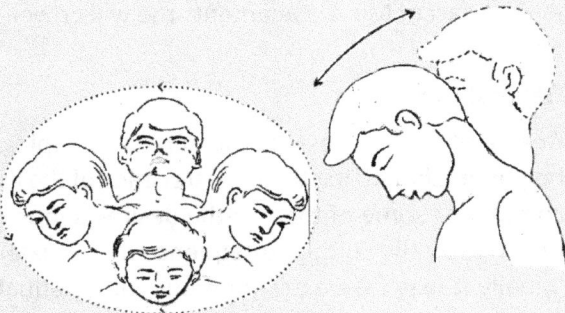
Figure 7

For Mouth: Open your mouth as wide as you can without any pain. Keep it open for few seconds, then close and relax in its normal state (Figure 8). Again open and so on. Repeat for 3 to 5 times. Then open the mouth and move the jaws from left to right and right to left 3 to 5 times.

For Eyes: Stand with your back, neck and head straight. Straighten the right arms at the shoulder level with fingers folded in a fist and thumb standing up. Focus on the tip of the thumb and start rotating the thumb clockwise (Figure 9). Move your eyeballs in the direction of the thumb. Then rotate the thumb in anti-clockwise direction. Repeat the same steps 5-10 times.

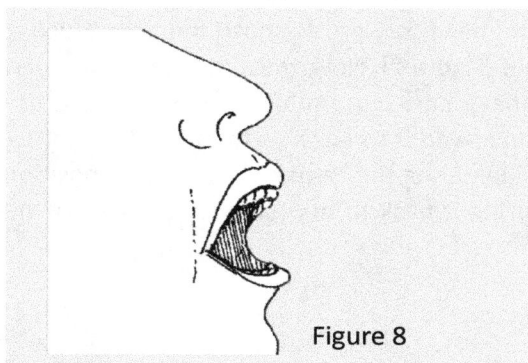
Figure 8

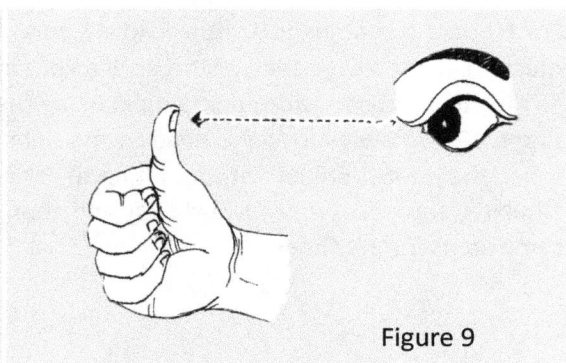
Figure 9

Pragya Yog

Pragya Yog involves all the three bodies (physical, subtle and causal) of a person. The Asan (physical exercise) rejuvenates body, Pranayam (breath control) strengthens mind and chanting in the heart of Mantra augments the will power. The sequence of exercises of this yoga is given below.

General Guidelines

Aasan refers to a specific posture for keeping the body healthy and active internally. The beginners should first try to master each of the listed asans one by one separately. Then attempt completing some of them in the desired sequence. Having mastered over the sub-sequences, one may try the complete sequence of the sixteen asans as described in the following section. Initially it may take extra time but with gradual practice one will be tuned up and complete round of these asans will be over only in about ten minutes.

The Sequence of *Asans*

Select peaceful, open and pure environment. Stand erect keeping your vision straight. Develop faith and inner feeling that the spiritual power of God is rejuvenating the body, mind and soul.

1. **Tadasan:** Stand on the toes. Raise both the hands upward while inhaling gradually and deeply. Look upwards to the sky. Hold your breath inside. This exercise helps adequate blood supply in the heart, stretching the spine backwards and thus giving it the much-needed rest. This practice instantly removes lethargy. **(Position 1)**

2. **Pad Hastasana:** Now bring both the hands downward from the posture of tadasan and exhale at the same slow and consistent pace and bow the head down to touch the knees, also attempt making the palms touch the floor. Hold your breath out for several seconds and come back to the normal standing posture. Practice of this *asan* removes gastric trouble and induces vital strength and reduces fat on the tummy. **(Position 2)**

3. **Vajrasan:** place the toes completely on the floor and set the haunches on the feet. Both the legs should be in closed contact. Keep the backbone erect and place the palms on the knees. Breathe normally during this posture. The back, neck and head should remain straight. Practising this asan for few minutes every day is helpful in maintaining good digestion and curing gastric trouble and constipation. It strengthens the muscles around stomach and protects from the problems of hernia. **(Position 3)**

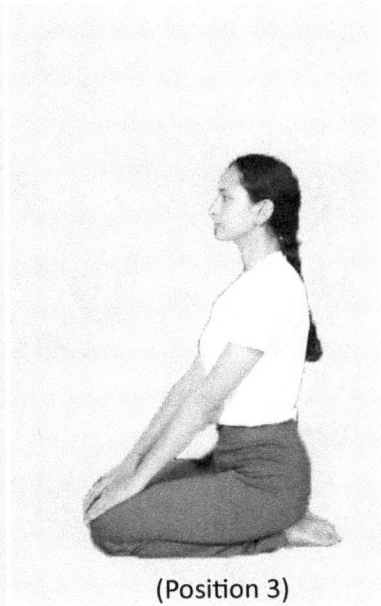

(Position 1)　　　(Position 2)　　　(Position 3)

4. **Ushtrasan:** Now get up slightly from the vajrasan. Stand on your knees with the toes touching the floor and the heels facing backwards. Almost simultaneously, bend backwards to place the palms on the heels from the backside. Inhale deeply while looking upwards. This will inflate your chest. Hold the breath in for few seconds. This *asan* stretches the abdomen, stomach, chest, and hands in a balanced way. Practice of this *asan* helps healing the problems of backache and makes the heart strong and augments the natural elasticity of the spinal column. **(Position 4)**

5. **Yogamudra:** Now exhale slowly and sit on your legs as in vajrasana at the same time, clench together both the palms at the back and stretch upwardly and place the head on the floor so that the chest and the stomach touch the thighs. Hold the breath out for few seconds. This posture further helps curing severe gastric troubles, setting the metabolic activities right and increasing the appetite. **(Position 5)**

6. **Ardh Tadasan:** Take deep breath. Being seated in the posture of vajrasan, raise both the arms and eyes upwards. Hold the breath inside and stretch the arms as much as you can without pain. Focus your eyes on the hands. This asan gives a natural and mild traction to the neck and allays the problems, if any, like Cervical Spondylitis. **(Position 6)**

(Position 4) (Position 5) (Position 6)

7. **Shashankasan:** Exhale at the same pace as inhalation in the preceding asan. Simultaneously, sit in the posture of vajrasan and keep both the arms stretched outwardly in front of the chest. Place the palms on the floor, bend from the waist to make the stomach touch the thighs and the head touch the floor. The arms should remain straight with palms touching the floor. Hold the breath outside for few seconds. This *asan* eliminates the problem of constipation and soothingly stretches the muscles within and between the anus and buttock regions. It relaxes the Sciatica nerves and also helps in regularizing the secretions from the adrenal gland. **(Position 7)**

8. **Bhujangasan:** Take deep breath and pull your waist upwards. Toes and palm should remain at the same place where these were in the previous posture but now the arms should stand straighten. The knees and thighs should touch the floor. Draw your chest and head upwards and raise the head like a snake's hood. Hold the breath inside and bend the head backwards slightly to stare the sky. This exercise is also recommended as a remedy against Cervical Spondylitis and several other problems of the spine or back. **(Position 8)**

9. **Tiryak Bhujangasan (left):** In the posture of bhujangasan, exhale slowing. Now take a deep breath and turn the neck towards the left and try looking at the heel of right foot. Then hold the breath for few seconds. With exhalation bring the head in the front. **(Position 9)**

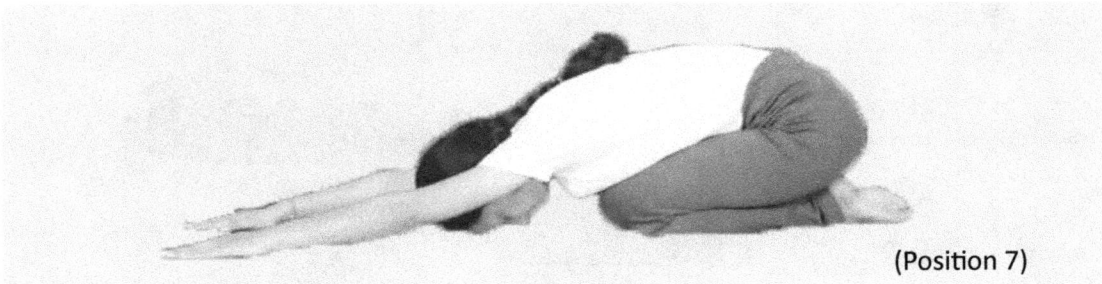

(Position 7)

(Position 8)

10. **Tiryak Bhujangasan (right):** Take deep breath and turn the neck towards the right to see the heel of the left foot. Hold the breath for few seconds and bring the head again in the front with exhalation. Practice of the tiryak bhujangasan enhances flexibility of the waist and augments the benefits of the bhujangasan. **(Position 10)**

11. **Shashankasan:** Now return to the posture of step 7. **(Position 11)**

12. **Ardh Tadasan:** Repeat step 6. **(Position 12)**

13. **Utkatasan:** After ardha tadasan in step 12, exhale slowly. With normal breathing sit on the toes. The heels should not touch the floor. Let the calves touch the thighs and knees touch the buttocks. Place both the palms on the knees. Bend the arms on elbows and keep the hands in front of the chest with palms placed on each other in the posture of Namaskar. Back, neck and head should be erect. Breathing should be deep and continued at a consistent pace. This *asan* gives strength to the calves and improves balance of the body. **(Position 13)**

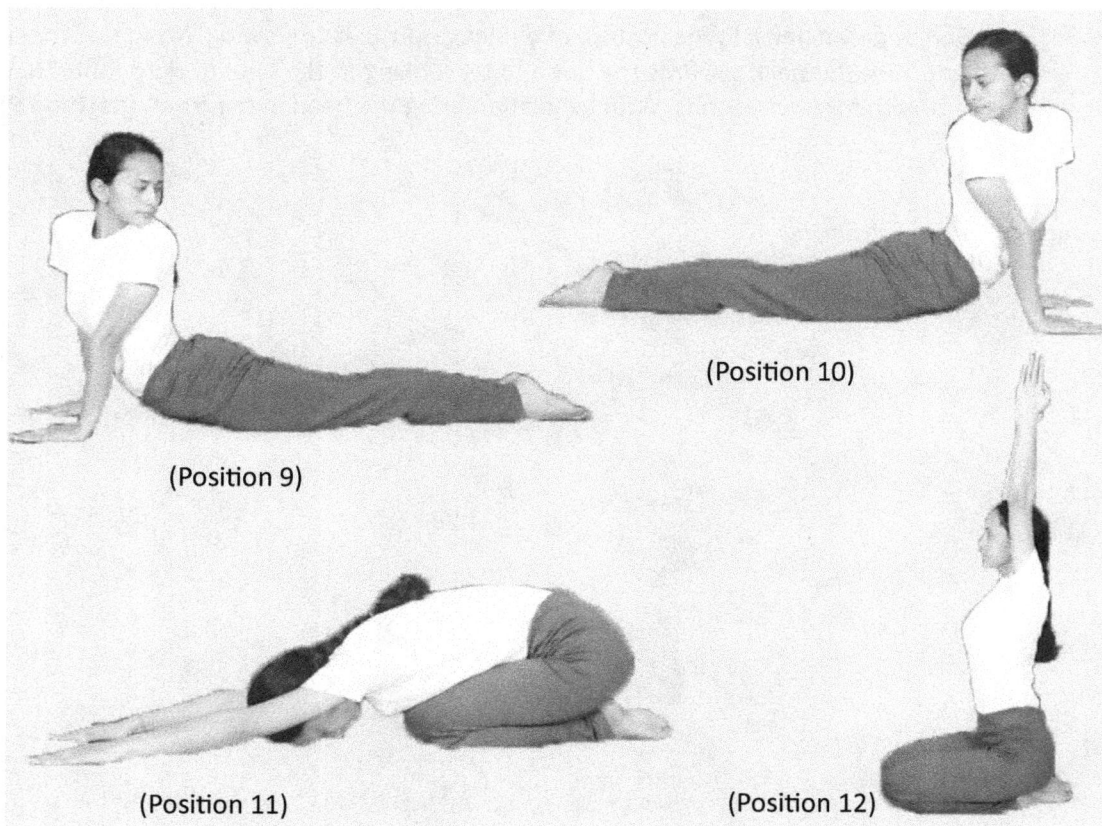

(Position 9)

(Position 10)

(Position 11)

(Position 12)

14. **Padhastasan:** Repeat step 2. **(Position 14)**

15. **Tadasan:** Stand on the toes. Raise both the hands upward while inhaling gradually and deeply. Look upwards to the sky. Hold your breath inside. This exercise helps adequate blood supply in the heart, stretching the spine backwards and thus giving it the much-needed rest. This practice instantly removes lethargy. **(Position 15)**

16. **Coming back to original position:** Inhale slowly and deeply, and stand straight with stretched chest. Place the arms upwards and bend the elbows above the shoulders in a posture as though you are holding a heavy rock on the hands. Hold the breath for few seconds with a feeling that your arms, shoulders, chest and whole body are empowered by new vital force. Now close the fists. Exhale slowly, bring the arms on the sides and stand straight in the posture of attention. Breathe normal in a relaxed mood. **(Position 16)**

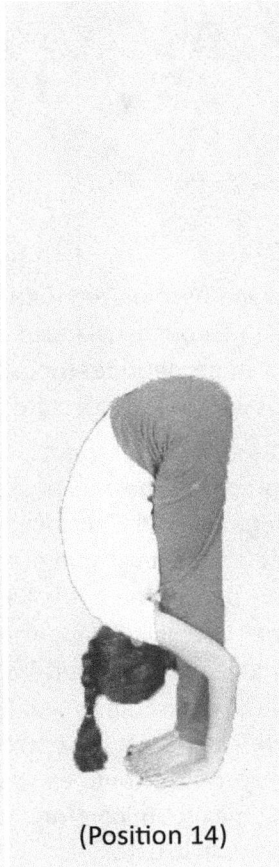

(Position 13)   (Position 14)   (Position 15)   (Position 16)

These sixteen steps complete one round of the Pragya Yoga asans. With gradual progress, one may complete 3 to 5 rounds every day. Adept practice of these everyday would help controlled movements for strengthening the nerves, muscles and different organs and regularizing the blood supply in all parts of the body.

Significance of Breathing in Yoga: Adequate and harmonized (with respect to body functions and the bioelectrical flows) supply of oxygen through balanced and deep breathing helps nourishing secretion and circulation of several neuropeptides (neuro-transmitters) and healthy activation of the endocrine (hormonal) glands which lead to a state of psychosomatic calm and peace.

Precautions: Irrespective of whether one practises these exercises in group or alone, one should follow certain disciplines that are essential for all kinds of yoga. It should be noted that an exercise should be practised only if one is able to do it without putting excessive pressure and devoid of any pain or unusual sensation in any part of the body. There should also be balance of forward, backward and sideways bending. Usually, pregnant woman, people who have undergone some surgery or suffering from injury are restrained from doing specific exercises. One should relax for some time (15-20 minutes) after doing yoga. In any case, nothing should be eaten or drunk for at least half-an hour before and after the exercises. Consumption of spicy or oily food should be avoided. All physical exercises should be practised by sitting, standing or lying down on a folded blanket or cloth for maximum comfort. In general, it is advisable to learn yoga under the supervision of an expert or instructor.

Common Rules of Yoga

1. Practice yoga for at least 15–20 minutes every day.

2. Perform yoga in fresh and open environment like park, garden etc.

3. Keep yourself positive and stress-free while doing yoga.

4. Best time for yoga are morning and evening. Practice yoga with empty bowel.

5. Do not perform yoga in hurry. The steps should be performed slowly and carefully.

6. Always breathe from nose while performing yoga. Take at least one minute rest before starting new exercise.

7. If you are suffering from any illness or pregnant, consult an expert before starting yoga.

8. Do not expect miracles. It removes stiffness and improves health slowly but effectively.

Miracle of Meditation

Human brain is an extremely wonderful cosmic computer. In a relaxed state, your mind is more open to new ideas and directions. Turbulent situations trigger powerful emotions in us. When emotions are on a high, the tendency is to react and be impulsive. A turbulent mind filled with such uncontrolled thoughts and emotions drains out the vital energy, leaving us completely tired, exhausted and frustrated. So how do we move from this turbulence to tranquillity? When the mind concentrates in one direction, a magnetic field is created which attracts the desired elements from the atmosphere. This process of focusing thoughts and emotions is called meditation. Meditation creates a unique hypo metabolic state, in which the metabolism is in an even deeper state of rest than during sleep. During sleep, oxygen consumption drops by 8 percent, but during meditation, it drops by 10 to 20 percent. Meditation is the only activity that reduces blood lactate, a marker of stress and anxiety.

When you meditate, your wandering mind starts settling down and focusing more on the task at hand. Focusing on breathing is known as mindfulness meditation. This is one of the simplest ways to meditate. We sit down and fix attention on our breath without any intervening thought. Accept all thoughts when you meditate. Let them come. Thoughts come and go away too. Observing this phenomenon will settle the mind. When you meditate, simply let go and enjoy. With this you will find the mind gradually coming to rest. As concentration develops, we begin to feel happy, relaxed and calm. Practice meditation for at least 20 minutes every day.

Some of the achievements of meditation are : • Enhanced memory • Muscular relaxation • Mental equipoise • Inner calmness • Increased awareness • Cheerfulness all the time

Sources

- http://kidshealth.org/teen/your_mind/body_image/body_image.html
- http://www.plannedparenthood.org/learn/body-image
- http://www.plannedparenthood.org/learn/relationships
- http://girlshealth.gov/body/sexuality/whywait.html
- http://www.advocatesforyouth.org/topics-issues/abstinence?task=view
- https://en.wikipedia.org/wiki/Adolescent_sexuality
- http://patient.info/health/the-male-reproductive-system
- http://www.womenshealth.gov/publications/our-publications/fact-sheet/menstruation.html
- http://www.quora.com/Does-maturbation-really-affect-your-health-if-you-do-it-on-a-daily-basis
- http://girlshealth.gov/body/sexuality/sti.html#what_are_stds
- http://www.mayoclinic.org/diseases-conditions/sexually-transmitted-diseases-stds/in-depth/std-symptoms/art-20047081?pg=1
- http://girlshealth.gov/body/reproductive/infections.html
- http://www.cancerresearchuk.org/health-professional/cancer-statistics/statistics-by-cancer-type/breast-cancer/survival#heading-One
- http://www.medicalnewstoday.com/articles/17131.php
- http://www.who.int/mediacentre/factsheets/fs110/en/
- http://www.onlymyhealth.com/foods-improve-sexual-health-1302587002
- http://www.menshealth.com/sex-md/better-sex-diet
- http://www.guttmacher.org/pubs/ib_std.html
- http://www.plannedparenthood.org/learn/sexuality
- whqlibdoc.who.int/hq/2010/WHO_RHR_HRP_10.22_eng.pdf
- unesdoc.unesco.org/images/0018/001832/183281e.pdf
- Straight Talk Foundation Annual Report 2008 available on http://www.straight-talk.org.ug
- http://www.soundvision.com/article/15-tips-for-victims-on-how-to-deal-with-sexual-assault-abuse-and-harassment-in-the-west
- http://www.eschooltoday.com/child-abuse/sexual-child-abuse/what-is-grooming-in-child-abuse.html
- http://www.nsopw.gov/en/Education/FactsStatistics?AspxAutoDetectCookieSupport=1
- https://www.rainn.org/get-information/types-of-sexual-assault/child-sexual-abuse
- http://www.kawarthasexualassaultcentre.com/the_facts
- http://www3.weforum.org/docs/WEF_GenderGap_Report_2013.pdf

- http://www.onlymyhealth.com/topic/sex-education
- http://www.ungift.org/knowledgehub/en/about/trafficking-of-children.html
- www.prb.org/pdf12/reproductivehealth-education-egypt.pdf
- http://www.who.int/reproductivehealth/en/
- http://www.unicef.org/teachers/protection/prevention.htm
- www.who.int/school_youth_health/media/en/family_life.pdf
- http://www.collective-evolution.com/2015/06/22/in-the-netherlands-sex-education-starts-in-kindergarten-heres-what-they-tell-them-why/
- www.escrh.eu/sites/escrh.eu/files/WHO_Standard_Sexuality_Education_0.pdf
- http://www.cdc.gov/reproductivehealth/unintendedpregnancy/contraception.htm
- http://www.plannedparenthood.org/learn/birth-control
- http://www.nhs.uk/Conditions/contraception-guide/Pages/contraception.aspx
- http://sexuality.about.com/od/contraception/ht/putoncondom.htm
- https://en.wikipedia.org/wiki/Birth_control
- http://girlshealth.gov/safety/school/index.html
- http://www.wikigreen.in/2014/06/hidden-spy-camera-types-features-how-to.html
- https://www.shelleylubben.com/shelleys-articles/current-porn-statistics-2014
- http://stoppornculture.org/about/about-the-issue/facts-and-figures-2/
- http://www.prweb.com/releases/2013/2/prweb10382404.htm
- http://www.mob76outlook.com/the-us-porn-industry-continues-to-get-bigger-and-bigger/
- http://www.forbes.com/2001/05/25/0524porn.html
- http://www.extremetech.com/computing/123929-just-how-big-are-porn-sites
- Vanessa Vega and Neil M. Malamuth, "Predicting Sexual Aggression: The Role of Pornography in the Context of General and Specific Risk Factors," *Aggressive Behavior*, Volume 33 (2007): pp. 104–117.
- E. Carmer, L. McFarlane, B. Parker, K. Soeken, C. Silva, and S. Reel. "Violent pornography and the abuse of women: Theory to practice," *Violence and Victims*, Volume 13, Number 4 (1998): pp. 319-332.
- Gene Abel, Mary Mittleman, and Judith Becker. "Sexual offenders: Results of assessment and recommendations for treatment," *in Clinical Criminology: The Assessment and Treatment of Criminal Behavior*, ed. Mark Ben-Aron, Stephen Hucker, and Christopher Webster, pp. 191-205 (Toronto: Clarke Institute of Psychiatry, 1985).
- https://www.shelleylubben.com/shelleys-articles/current-porn-statistics-2014
- http://www.covenanteyes.com/2011/09/07/the-connections-between-pornography-and-sex-trafficking/
- http://fightthenewdrug.org/porns-dirty-little-secret/#sthash.yNKM8Cuo.dpbs
- Catherine Itzin, "Pornography and the Organization of Intrafamilial and Extrafamilial Child Sexual Abuse: Developing a Conceptual Model." Child Abuse Review, Vol. 10 (2001): pp. 35–48. Liz Kelly, "Weasel words: paedophiles and the cycle of abuse," Trouble and Strife, volume 33 (1996): pp.

44–49.

- National Center for Missing & Exploited Children. Internet Sex Crimes Against Minors: The Response of Law Enforcement. Virginia: National Center for Missing & Exploited Children, 2003.
- Top Ten Reviews, 2005.
- http://erlc.com/issues/quick-facts/por/
- The CP80 Foundation
- http://en.wikipedia.org/wiki/Child_pornography
- http://www.cybercellmumbai.gov.in/html/cyber-crimes/child-pornography.html
- http://www.independent.co.uk/life-style/health-and-families/health-news/pornography-addiction-leads-to-same-brain-activity-as-alcoholism-or-drug-abuse-study-shows-8832708.html
- http://scienceblogs.com/cortex/2009/08/24/porn-and-mirror-neurons/Fire: stimulated enough to carry the current (action potential)
- http://www.ncbi.nlm.nih.gov/pubmed/11572966
- http://bigthink.com/going-mental/is-your-brain-addicted-to-porn
- http://www.toppaidpornsite.com/pornography-really-only-adults/
- https://www.netnanny.com/assets/brochures/FightTheNewDrug-5-Tips.pdf
- https://www.youtube.com/watch?v=-5PZ_Bh-M6o
- www.struttcentral.com
- http://edition.cnn.com/2013/02/27/health/cyberbullying-online-bully-victims/
- http://www.protectkids.com/effects/harms.htm
- http://www.nlm.nih.gov/medlineplus/mentalhealth.html
- http://www.mentalhelp.net/poc/view_doc.php?type=doc&id=54920&cn=117
- http://familydoctor.org/familydoctor/en/prevention-wellness/emotional-wellbeing/mental-health/mind-body-connection-how-your-emotions-affect-your-health.printerview.all.html
- http://www.mentalhealthamerica.net/conditions/healthy-diet-eating-mental-health-mind
- https://www.psychologytoday.com/blog/real-healing/201301/healthy-gut-healthy-mind-5-foods-improve-mental-health
- http://www.boredpanda.com/love-facts-list/

Our inspiration...

Pandit Sriram Sharma Acharya, a pioneer of spiritual renaissance was born on 20th September 1911, in Anwalkheda village, Agra District, India. A sage, a visionary and a reformer, Acharyaji initiated 100 points social reformation program, Yug Nirman Yojna, established over 3000 social reform centers, lived a disciplined life of devout austerity and attained spiritual eminence.

Acharyaji dedicated his life, with increasing focus as it progressed, to launch a massive popular movement for the sake of reviving the spiritual traditions that had formed the foundations of ancestral Indian culture. His wife, Mata Bhagwati Devi Sharma, came in Acharyaji's life in 1943 and they dedicatedly pursued the noble mission for arousal of human glory and revival of divine culture.

Acharyaji initiated his social upliftment work from birthplace Anwalkheda; established Gayatri Tapobhumi, Mathura, where *Gayatri Pariwar* came into existence. This has now expanded across globe beyond the barriers of religion, creed, caste, sex or socioeconomic status. In 1971, Acharyaji instituted *Gayatri Pariwar* fraternity at Shantikunj, Haridwar for moral and spiritual awakening and training.

Throughout his life, Acharyaji owned only two sets of clothes. Upon the basis of his simplicity was established the integrity of a movement that would renounce the addictions of modern life. He took part in the struggle for Indian independence as a volunteer, went jail a number of times and embarked upon the task of social and moral upliftment through spiritual means. He wrote discourses on every aspect of human culture and well-being that are translated in 13 languages. Acharyaji translated the entire Vedic literature and accomplished a feat of writing more than 3000 books on all aspects of life. His literature is a wonderful confluence of sagacity, versatility and lucidity. His writings seem to carry a vital force that induces vibrant thoughts and engrossing joy in the reader's mind and heart. Some of his books deal with in-depth and rare piece of knowledge in simple language, while some provide practical solutions to day-to-day problems, and some others focus at resolving global challenges.

Acharya Sriram Sharma, Great devotee of *Gayatri* lived an ideal life for 80 years and voluntarily shed his physical sheath on *Gayatri Jayanti*, 2nd June 1990 magnifying his sublime powers up to the higher realms of divinity in order to enlighten the subtle world of people's thoughts and sentiments.

www.ingramcontent.com/pod-product-compliance
Lightning Source LLC
Chambersburg PA
CBHW080613270326
41928CB00016B/3043